MEDITATION
AND
THE BIBLE

BY

ARYEH KAPLAN

MEDITATION

AND

THE BIBLE

BY

ARYEH KAPLAN

SAMUEL WEISER, INC.
York Beach, Maine

First published in 1978 by
Samuel Weiser, Inc.
Box 612
York Beach, Maine 03910

First paper edition, 1988

ISBN 0-87728-617-5

Library of Congress Catalog Card Number: 84-050350

Printed in the United States of America

Contents

ACKNOWLEDGMENTS

Dr. Perle Epstein.

Library of Jewish Theological Seminary of America,
New York, New York,
particularly to Ms. Susan Young
and Mr. Micha Falk Oppenheim.

Hebrew University Libraries,
Jerusalem.

Bodleian Library,
Oxford, England.

Biblioteque Nationale,
Paris, France.

British Museum,
London, England.

Biblioteca Apostolica Vatican,
Vatican City.

Columbia University Library
Manuscript Division
New York, New York.

Lenin State Library
Guenzburg Collection
Moscow.

Introduction

ONE OF THE GREATEST MYSTERIES of the Bible involves the
methods used by the prophets to attain their unique states of
consciousness. Almost all of the Bible was authored by these
prophets while in such higher states, but virtually nothing is
known about how they were attained. In the actual text of the
Bible, very little is said about the methods, and the few relevant passages that do exist are difficult to understand and
require adequate interpretation. But unless their methods are
known, it is difficult to put the teachings of the prophets of the
Bible in their proper context, and consequently, many other
concepts found in this sacred book are apt to be understood
inadequately.

There are dangers and pitfalls in any attempt to shed new
light on the Bible, and throughout the years, people have
attempted to read the most outlandish ideas into the sacred
text. It is therefore most important to explore the classical
Judaic traditions and commentaries to see if they shed any
light on the matter.

In general, there are two methods through which one can
attain a mystical state or a higher level of consciousness, meditation and drugs. While some writers have tried to demonstrate that the prophets engaged in drug experiences, there is
no objective evidence, either from the Biblical text or from the
classical literature, that such substances were involved.

With regard to meditation, the precise opposite is true. As
soon as we learn to understand the vocabulary, we find many
references in the literature to Biblical meditation, and as re-
cently as two hundred years ago we find it discussed in detail.
One reason why this is not generally recognized is because all
of this literature is in Hebrew, and, since meditation is for all
practical purposes no longer practiced in Jewish circles, the

meaning of the vocabulary associated with it has been forgotten.

An important task of this book, therefore, will be to relearn the vocabulary used in classical Hebraic literature to describe the various meditative methods. This is very important, since the most frequently used Hebrew word for meditation is generally not recognized as such, and most translators render it incorrectly, completely losing the meaning of relevant texts. Even individuals with otherwise excellent scholarly credentials often misinterpret important writings, not realizing that they are referring to meditation solely because the correct translation of the relevant words is not known.

In the first section of this book, we will explore the relevant terminology, quoting numerous sources which, in context, unambiguously demonstrate the meaning of these words. In this section, we remain on firm ground, not resorting to any conjecture whatsoever. It appears that the main reason why the meanings of these words is not generally recognized is simply because no one ever went to the trouble to systematically explore all the sources where they are quoted.

The role of meditative techniques becomes all the more evident when one realizes the great extent to which they are discussed in the Kabbalistic literature. Unfortunately, most of this remains in unpublished manuscript, but here also, there is enough published material to provide a clear picture.

In Kabbalistic literature, we find considerable use of mantra-type meditation, where one repeats certain phrases, syllables, or divine names over and over in order to attain a meditative state. Another important method is that of Unifications *(Yichudim),* where the individual meditates on certain mystical names and letters, combining and unifying them in a prescribed manner. All of this will be presented in a companion to this volume, entitled *Meditation and Kabbalah.*

In the second section of this book, we will explore the various prophetic methods and experiences, both from the Biblical text itself and from the viewpoint of its classical commentaries. As this is explored in a systematic manner, some insight is also gained into the meditative methods used by the great prophets of Israel.

Most speculative is the third section, where an attempt is made to reconstruct the Biblical vocabulary used to describe the various meditative and mystical states. Here we switch gears, moving from the teachings of the philosophers and Kabbalists to those of the great Hebrew philologists. A study is made, both from context and from comparative philology and etymology, attempting to identify and interpret the various words that the Bible uses to describe meditative methods and higher states of consciousness.

Due to the fact that much of the material in this book may seem somewhat controversial, we will clearly stress the extent that it is discussed in classical Judaic literature. Wherever practical, we will quote from the primary sources, often presenting them for the first time in the English language. All translations in this book have been made by the author.

It is hoped and intended that this brief study will open an avenue for further research into the meaning of the Bible, as well as the significance of the prophetic experience, which is its basis. While this treatment is far from complete, it should provide a key for those who wish to open the inner doors and further explore these mysteries.

ARYEH KAPLAN
23 Adar II, 5736

PART ONE

The Traditions

1

Internal Isolation

Many people are initially surprised to discover that meditation plays any role whatsoever in Biblical teachings. It is a subject not often discussed in this context, and many individuals who are otherwise knowledgeable in Biblical thought are hardly aware that numerous important classical Judaic commentators interpret certain passages as referring to meditative experiences. One important reason for this is that such practices have not been in use since the great Hasidic renaissance almost two centuries ago. Where the experience itself is not known, the meaning of words used to describe it also becomes forgotten, and the entire vocabulary is lost.

Therefore, before the concept of meditation as it occurs in Hebraic sources can adequately be discussed, a basic vocabulary must be developed. There are a few words in the Bible itself that apparently have important connotations with regard to meditative states of unconsciousness, but these expressions are not used in this context in post-Biblical literature.

There is, however, one word that is consistently used as a term for meditation, by commentators, philosophers and Kabbalists. The one word which most often denotes meditation is

Hitbodedut (הִתְבּוֹדְדוּת). The verb, "to meditate," is represented by the word *Hitboded* (הִתְבּוֹדֵד).

The word *Hitboded* is derived from the root *Baded* (בדד), meaning "to be alone." Literally, then, *Hitbodedut* actually means self-isolation, and in some cases, it actually means nothing more than physical seclusion and isolation.[1] In many other places, however, it is used to denote a state of consciousness involving the isolation of the self, that is, the isolation of the individual's most basic essence.

Thus, when discussed in a Kabbalistic context, the word *Hitbodedut* means much more than mere physical isolation. It refers to a kind of internal isolation, where the individual mentally isolates his essence from his thoughts. One of the greatest of all Kabbalists, Rabbi Chaim Vital (1543-1620), often speaks of such mental seclusion, saying that "one must seclude himself *(hitboded)* in his thoughts to the ultimate degree." [2] In doing so, one separates his soul from the body to such a degree that he no longer feels any relationship to his physical self. The soul is thus isolated, and as Rabbi Chaim Vital concludes, "the more one separates himself from the physical, the greater will be his perception."

This state of mental seclusion is very important to the prophetic experience. There is considerable discussion of this, but the clearest description of this state is presented by Rabbi Levi ben Gershon (1288–1344), a major Jewish philosopher, often known as Gersonides or simply "the Ralbag." He clearly writes that the receiving of prophetic revelation "requires the isolation *(hitbodedut)* of the consciousness from the imagination, or of both of these from the other perceptive mental faculties." [3]

The Ralbag is speaking of the meditative state, which he describes as the isolation of the consciousness to an extent where it is no longer disturbed by the imagination. The imagination to which he refers is the normal reverie involving the stream of consciousness and visual imagery that is experienced when all the other senses are shut off. It is from this that the intellect must be isolated, until the individual enters a state of pure consciousness, disturbed by neither reverie nor visual imagery. This is a normal definition of the meditative state, and it is the end result of all successful meditation. In order to attain this, the individual must isolate both the consciousness and the imagination from the other perceptive faculties of the mind.

In order to understand this more fully, we must realize that the human brain, marvelous organ that it appears to be, is still usually very inefficient as a thinking device. Henri Bergson has suggested that one of the main functions of the brain and nervous system may be to eliminate activity and awareness, rather than to produce it.

Aldous Huxley quotes Prof. C.D. Broad's comments on this.[4] He states that every person has an innate capability of remembering everything that has ever happened to him and of perceiving all events that surround him. If all this information poured into our minds at once, however, it would completely overwhelm us, so the function of the brain and nervous system is to protect us and prevent us from being overwhelmed and confused by the vast amount of information that reaches our sense organs. They shut out most of what we perceive and remember, eliminating all that would confuse us, so that only the small, special selection that is useful is allowed to remain.

If this is true of visions in the physical world, it would be even more true of the extramundane. If an ordinary person were constantly able to visualize the spiritual domain, it would be absolutely impossible for him to function on a physical plane. Although the human mind has powers of perception and concentration that we cannot even begin to imagine, our main business is to survive at all costs. To make survival possible, all of our mind's capabilities must be funneled through the reducing valve of the brain.

Some researchers are studying this effect, maintaining that this reducing-valve effect may be very similar to the jamming equipment used to block out offensive radio broadcasts. The brain constantly produces a kind of static, cutting down our perception and reducing our mental activity.

This static can actually be seen. When you close your eyes, you see all sorts of random pictures flashing through your mind. It is impossible to concentrate on any one of them for more than an instant, and each image is obscured by a host of others superimposed over it. This static can even be seen when the eyes are open, but we usually ignore these images, since they are very faint compared to our visual perception. Still, this static reduces our perception, both of the world around us and of ourselves. Even more so, it makes it impossible to perceive the spiritual domain in any manner whatsoever, at least while in a normal state of consciousness.

One of the important purposes of meditation, then, is to eliminate this and similar static. As the Ralbag explains, one does this by isolating the essence of one's consciousness from the imagination, which is the part of the mind that produces such mental static. When one accomplishes this, he can see and understand things much more clearly, and even gain a perception of the spiritual domain.

2

Abraham Maimonides

Although many authors use the term *Hitbodedut* to refer to the meditative state, the word is most often used for the actual act of meditation, and many examples of this are found in the Kabbalistic literature. The clearest expression of this, however, is found in the writings of Rabbi Abraham Maimonides (1186–1237), son of the famed philosopher, codifier and physician, Moses Maimonides.[5]

Rabbi Abraham Maimonides writes that there are two types of isolation *(hitbodedut)*, external and internal. External isolation is nothing more than physical seclusion, but internal isolation refers to the meditative process, where one isolates himself both spiritually and mentally.

Such meditation is seen as the highest of all practices, being the method used by the prophets to attain their revelation. The prophets frequently engaged in physical seclusion, but the main purpose of such external isolation was as preparation for internal isolation or meditation, which brought one to the highest step on the ladder of revelation. Such a state of internal isolation is seen, not only as a means to attain revelation, but as actually being the revelation itself.

A number of Biblical verses are seen by Rabbi Abraham as referring to such a meditative state. It is the perfection from within the heart for which King David prayed when he said, "A pure heart create for me, O God" *(Psalm 51:12)*. It was also the attainment of Aseph, regarding which he sang, "My flesh and heart fade away, while God becomes the Rock of my heart and my portion forever" *(Psalm 73:26)*. These verses refer to the purity of the mind and heart, when they are cleansed of all things other than the Divine. When a person attains such a state, the Divine Essence is actually seen as entering the mind and dwelling in it.

The method through which this is attained is also clearly described: "This level is achieved through a cessation of activity on the part of the perceptive faculty, completely, or at least for the most part, divorcing it from the soul. The motivating force of the consciousness is thus divorced from all worldly concepts and is inclined toward the Divine. The intellect then becomes enveloped in the Divine, and the imagination which is associated with the meditative faculty becomes activated through contemplation in God's creation, gazing at the mighty things that bear witness to their Creator."

The main method of meditation as outlined by Rabbi Abraham, thus involves the contemplation of nature. A person can contemplate the greatness of the sea, marveling at the many creatures that live in it. One can gaze at a clear night sky, allowing his mind to be completely absorbed by the glory of the stars. Through such intense contemplation, one can attain a meditative state directed toward the Divine.

This is seen as the level of Aseph, one of the co-authors of the Psalms, who purified his heart and mind, cleansing it of all things other than the Divine. It is regarding this state that he said, "My flesh and heart fade away." When he divorced his consciousness from everything but God, he said, "Who have I in heaven? And with You, I have no desire on earth" *(Psalm 73:25)*.

Although the entire psalm is not discussed, many other verses can readily be seen to refer to the meditative state, and indeed, it is so interpreted by some of the most important classical Judaic commentators.[6] It is therefore enlightening to look at the entire last part of this psalm and see the two quoted verses in context:

I am continually with You,
  You have grasped my right hand.
With Your counsel You guide me,
  After glory You take me.
Who have I in heaven?
  With You, I have no desire on earth.
My flesh and heart fade away,
  God becomes the Rock of my heart,
  My portion forever. . . .
For me, closeness to God is good,
  I have placed my essence in God my Lord,
  To express all Your transcendence.

Numerous other Biblical verses are also interpreted in this light. Thus, regarding the inclination of his consciousness toward the Divine, the prophet Isaiah said, "Your name and Your remembrance are the desire of my soul; My soul longs for You by night, also my spirit within me dawns forth to You" *(Isaiah 26:8,9).*[7] The Psalmist likewise said, "My soul thirsts for You, my flesh pines for You" *(Psalms 63:2),* and in another place, "My soul cleaves after You" *(Psalms 63:9).*

Another important point discussed by Rabbi Abraham is that all ego and sensation must be restrained before the meditative faculty can function. An example of this is seen in Elisha's advice to Gehazi: "If you meet a man, do not bless him, and if a man blesses you, do not answer him" *(2 Kings* 4:29). This is particularly noteworthy, since it seems to indicate that a certain degree of stoicism is necessary before one can adequately engage in meditation, a concept that is discussed at length by the Kabbalists.[8]

In order to attain the meditative state which unifies man and God, the prophets and their disciples would make use of various types of music and song. Rabbi Abraham writes that this would motivate the consciousness toward God, and purify one's inner being of all external thoughts. There are a number of verses that mention this, one of the clearest being what is written with regard to the Temple service, "David and his overseers singled out the sons of Asaph, Heman and Jeduthun, who would prophesy with harps, lutes and cymbols" *(1 Chronicles* 25:1).[9]

In order to be able to attain internal isolation, the prophets and their disciples also engaged in external isolation, seclud-

ing themselves from the general populace. They were then not
disturbed by the mundane affairs of the multitudes, and could
meditate on God and His works without interruption. Such
isolation could be partial and temporary, or it could be total,
where the individual secluded himself in unpopulated areas
such as deserts and mountains. Rabbi Abraham notes that
such seclusion is often mentioned in the careers of the prophets
and their disciples. It is also for this reason that many patriarchs and prophets worked as shepherds, where they could
be alone in the fields for long periods of time.

During such periods of isolation, the prophet would contemplate the sky and the mountains, as well as all the rest of
God's works, drawing his mind to their Creator. According to
Rabbi Abraham, this is the meaning of King David's statement, "How weighty are Your meditations, O God, how great is
their sum, if I could count them, they would outnumber the
sands" *(Psalms 139:17,18)*. One becomes so immersed in his
contemplation that he enters a state of trance and mental
quietude, perceiving the unity of God like one who can actually
sense it. When a person who has attained such a state is
aroused, the spell of this unity remains with him, and David
thus concludes, "I awakened and I was still with You" *(Psalms
139:18)*.[10]

The best time for such meditation is at midnight or before
dawn. Rabbi Abraham finds allusions for this in such verses as,
"Rise, meditate in the night, at the beginning of the watches"
(Lamentations 2:19).[11] King David likewise said, "Before my
eyes are the night-watches, when I meditate on Your word"
(Psalms 119:148). The younger Maimonides also speaks of
some individuals who attempt to go without sleep completely,
attempting to emulate the devotion described in the verse, "I
will not give sleep to my eyes, nor slumber to my eyelids"
(Lamentations 132:4).

Of great importance is Rabbi Abraham's discussion of the
Moslem dervishes or Sufis, with whom he was apparently quite
familiar. He describes a practice of one of their sects, where
individuals would meditate in dark places, secluding themselves to such an extent that their sense of sight degenerated
and they could no longer discern between light and darkness.
In order for an individual to engage in such practices, he notes,

one must be motivated by a strong inner light so as not to be troubled by external darkness. A certain "Abraham the Saint" is quoted as discussing such meditation in dark places and applying to it the verse, "Who among you fears God, obeying the voice of His servants? Such a man walks in darkness without any light, he trusts in the Lord and depends on his God" *(Isaiah 50:10).*

Even though meditation is best accomplished when one is secluded, an individual on an advanced spiritual level can engage in it any time. The younger Maimonides thus quotes a blessing frequently used by the great sages, "May God grant your portion among the ones who delight in seclusion, whose soul is isolated even among many people."

Besides their value in providing important insights into meditation in general, these writings of Rabbi Abraham Maimonides are also extremely valuable because of the light that they shed on the writings of his father, the famed Moses Maimonides. Although the son is not as well known, the father was one of the greatest of all Judaic thinkers, who distilled all earlier teachings and influenced virtually every later writer.

From here, we clearly see that when Maimonides uses the term *Hitboded,* he is actually speaking of meditation, a fact that has escaped the notice of almost every translator. A good example of such usage can be found in a letter that the elder Maimonides writes to his son Abraham. He says, "The first two covenants (circumcision and the Torah) are upheld through the third, which is the Sabbath. The goal of all three is the purification of the soul, methodology, withdrawal, as well as meditation *(hitbodedut)* toward God." [12]

But what is even more important is the fact that Maimonides speaks of *Hitbodedut* with respect to the prophets, saying that it was one of the important techniques through which they attained their high level.[13] From his son's writings, we clearly see that this is speaking of meditation. I do not know of a single translator, however, who appears to be aware of this fact.

This also sheds light on an important teaching regarding meditation that is found in Maimonides' *Guide to the Perplexed.* Since we know the meaning of the word *hitbodedut,* we can now translate it correctly.[14]

◇ ◇ ◇

It is written, "Love the Lord your God, and serve Him with all
your heart and with all your soul" *(Deuteronomy 11:13)*. We
have already demonstrated numerous times that the love of
God is identical with one's perception of Him. As a result of this
love, one is led to a state of worship which our sages call
"service of the heart."

In my opinion, this means that one should concentrate all
of his thoughts on the First Intellect, meditating *(hitboded)* on
it according to his ability.

·   ·   ·   ·

It has thus been demonstrated that one's aim, after having
attained enlightenment, should be to give oneself over to [God]
and make his intellect yearn for Him at all times. In most
cases, this is accomplished through seclusion and isolation.
Every pious individual should therefore strive for seclusion
and meditation *(hitbodedut),* not associating with others except when absolutely necessary.

·   ·   ·   ·

The pious were therefore particular to minimize the time
when they could not reflect on God's name. And they cautioned
others, saying, "Let not your minds be vacant from reflections
on God." In the same sense, King David said, "I have set God
before me always, He is at my right hand, I shall not be moved"
(Psalms 16:8). What he meant was, "I do not turn my thoughts
away from God — He is like my right hand, which I do not
forget for even an instant because of the ease of its motions.
Therefore, I shall not be moved — I shall not fall."

◇ ◇ ◇

SOURCES

If these were the only places where the term *hitbodedut* was
used to refer to meditation, one could easily dismiss them as
being anomalous. However, throughout the length and

breadth of Judaic literature the word is used, and, in context, it clearly refers to meditation. The earliest reference that we have found dates from close to a thousand years ago, and in almost every generation, there is some discussion of the subject.

The selections provided here are a literal translation of the words of their authors, presented here for the first time in English. For the most part, these quotations speak for themselves, providing important insight into the role of meditation in Judaic thought in general, without need of additional comment.

◇ ◇ ◇

God arranged the order of creation so that all things are bound to each other. The direction of events in the lower world depends on entities above them, as our sages teach, "There is no blade of grass in the world below that does not have an angel over it, striking it and telling it to grow." [15]

Human souls are also bound to higher levels, and therefore, when a perfect individual becomes involved in meditation *(hitbodedut)* upon wisdom, it is possible for him to predict future events. As a result of his deep meditation, his consciousness and mind fall into a trance, and through his deep probing of the mysteries of existence, he reaches the First Cause. The faculties of his heart then become like the Urim and Thumim, mystically bound to the angels in heaven, and he becomes attached to the Ultimate Good.

> *Hai Gaon (939–1038),*
> *Religious Leader and Mystic.*[16]

◇ ◇ ◇

On the six weekdays, the soul of the enlightened meditates *(hitboded)* on mundane affairs. But on the Sabbath, it must meditate to understand the works of God and His miracles.

> *Abraham Ibn Ezra (1089–1164),*
> *Philosopher, Mystic and Poet.*[17]

◇ ◇ ◇

In the souls of some individuals there exists the power of
prophecy, through which they can predict the future. No one
knows how this comes to them, but they meditate *(hitboded)*,
and a spirit comes and reveals the future to them.

> *Moses ben Nachman (Ramban:*
> *1194–1270),*
> *Legalist, Commentator and Mystic.*[18]

◇ ◇ ◇

It is taught that one who prays must concentrate his heart.
. . . One must concentrate on the words tha, leave his lips,
depicting the Divine Presence right in front of him, as it is
written, "I have placed God before me at all times" *(Psalms
16:8).* He must arouse his concentration, removing all disturbing thoughts so that his mind and concentration in prayer
remain pure. . . .

This was the way of the saints and men of deed. They
would meditate *(hitboded),* concentrating on their prayer until
they reached a level where they divested themselves of the
physical and were overcome by the spiritual. In this manner,
they were able to reach a level close to that of prophecy.

> *Rabbi Jacob ben Asher (1270–1343),*
> *Legal Codifier.*[19]

◇ ◇ ◇

The Talmud teaches that [after he was excommunicated by
Rabban Gamaliel,] Rabbi Eliezer's wife would not let him
"fall on his face" [in prayer, lest he kill Rabban Gamaliel].
This means that she disturbed him and would not let him
meditate *(hitboded).* Through such meditation, a person can
attach himself to the "proper place," and thus bring about
wonders and miracles.

> *Rabbi Shem Tov ibn Shaprut*
> *(1330–1400),*
> *Philosopher.*[20]

◇ ◇ ◇

God's thoughts are infinite, and regarding them, King David said, "If I would count them, they would outnumber the sands" *(Psalms 139:18)*. Still, in God [all these perfections are seen as] an absolute unity, as he adds, "For Him, there is unity in them" *(Psalms 139:16)*.

[King David concludes, "I awakened and was still with you." Here he is saying,] "When I was aroused from my meditation *(hitbodedut)* on [these perfections], I found that 'I am still with You,' since they are not something that is separated from You."

> *Rabbi Joseph Albo (1380–1435),*
> *Philosopher.*[21]

◇ ◇ ◇

I have at hand some response that one of the early codifiers received from heaven after asking in a proper manner. He did so through meditation *(hitbodedut)*, prayer, and the utterance of Divine Names, and thus received a reply to his questions.

> *Rabbi David ben Zimra (Radbaz:*
> *1470–1572),*
> *Legalist and Mystic.*[22]

◇ ◇ ◇

All the discussion regarding fasting and self mortification found in the earlier texts only apply to one who is not steadily involved in the study of the Torah. But when a person's main occupation is the Torah, and when he knows wisdom and fears God, he should not weaken himself and diminish his studies. This, then, is his rectification:

One day a week, separate yourself from all people and meditate *(hitboded)* upon God. Bind your thoughts to Him, just as if you were speaking to Him on the Day of Judgment. Speak to God softly, like a slave to his master, or a child to his parent.

> *Rabbi Isaac Luria (The Ari: 1534-1572),*
> *Master Kabbalist.*[23]

◇ ◇ ◇

The Talmud teaches that the early saints would wait an hour before praying in order to concentrate their thoughts upon God. The commentaries explain that this means that they would empty their minds of all mundane thoughts, and would bind their consciousness to the Master of all, with fear and love.

[These saints would then pray for an hour, and finally wait another hour after their prayers, so that they would spend a total of three hours on each of the three daily services.] It thus came out that they would take off a total of nine hours each day from their sacred studies in order to engage in meditation *(hitbodedut),* binding themselves [to God]. The Light of the Divine Presence would appear over their heads as if it were spread around them, with them sitting in the midst of the Light.

I found this in an old manuscript from the early mystics.

> *Rabbi Elazar Alkazri (1522–1600),*
> *Moralist and Mystic.*[24]

◇ ◇ ◇

Poets often speak of themselves as if they were referring to other individuals. [Jacob thus said,] "Gather around and listen, O sons of Jacob" *(Genesis 49:2).* [Baalam himself likewise said,] "Thus says Baalam, the son of Beor" *(Numbers 24:3).* [Deborah sang,], "Awake, awake, Deborah" *(Judges 5:12).* There are many similar cases.

This is because of their deep meditation *(hitbodedut),* where the mind elevates itself and the body remains as if it were devoid of the soul. It therefore appears to these individuals as if they themselves are another person. . . .

Occasionally we find that when they author their songs, poets attain a state of ecstasy where they lose all sensation. This is all because of their deep meditation.

> *Rabbi Emanuel Frances (1610–1710),*
> *Poet and Philosopher.*[25]

◇ ◇ ◇

One should constantly meditate *(hitboded)* on the Divine Presence. He should have no other thought in his mind other than his love [of God, seeking that the Divine Presence] should attach itself to him. In his mind he should constantly repeat, "When will I be worthy that the Light of the Divine Presence should dwell within me?"

Rabbi Israel Baal Shem Tov (1698–1760),
Founder of Hasidism.[26]

◇ ◇ ◇

The root of everything is meditation *(hitbodedut)*. It is a very great and lofty concept, making a person worthy of all holiness. . . . When a person meditates, he is clothed with holiness. . . . When one meditates, he is also attached to God, even with regard to his mundane bodily needs.

Rabbi Chaim Yosef David Azzulai
(The Chida: 1724–1806),
Sephardic leader and Kabbalist.[27]

◇ ◇ ◇

One must include himself in God's unity, which is the Imperative Existence. A person cannot be worthy of this, however, unless he nullifies his ego, and it is impossible to accomplish this without meditation *(hitbodedut)*. When a person meditates and expresses his thoughts before God, he can be worthy of nullifying all desires and evil traits, so that he becomes worthy of nullifying his entire physical being, thus becoming included in his Root.

Rabbi Nachman of Breslov (1772–1810),
Hasidic Master.[28]

3

Enlightenment

From these sources, it is evident that the concept of meditation was well known among the Judaic philosophers and Kabbalists, and that the term most often used to express this concept is *Hitbodedut*. While the philosophers often speak of unstructured meditation involving God and His creation, the Kabbalistic schools advocated more formal, structured ways of meditation.

The goal of meditation, especially as described by the Kabbalistic masters, is to attain enlightenment. In Hebrew, the word most often used to describe such enlightenment is *Ruach HaKodesh,* which can literally be translated as "Holy Spirit." It is this term that is consistently used by all Hebrew writers.

Although this term occurs in a number of places in the Bible, there is one place where this connotation is evident. In one of the Psalms, King David prays: *(Psalms 51:12–14):*

A pure heart, create for me, O God,
   A proper spirit, renew in me.
Cast me not away from Your presence,
   And take not Your *Holy Spirit* from me.
Return to me the joy of Your salvation,
   And let a willing spirit uphold me.

As we have seen, Rabbi Abraham Maimonides explains that the "pure heart" for which King David prayed refers to a heart and mind cleansed of all external thoughts through intense meditation. David had said this Psalm after he had been rebuked by the prophet Nathan because of his affair with Bathsheba. Prior to this, David had been on a very high spiritual level, but as a result of this affair, this enlightenment had been taken from him. He was now praying that he should once again have a "pure heart," and that God not take away from him the enlightenment which is *Ruach HaKodesh*.

The level of enlightenment implied by *Ruach HaKodesh* involves a clarity of understanding, an enhancement of perception, an awareness of the spiritual, and often, a complete change of personality. While in its lowest state, *Ruach HaKodesh* consists of general enlightenment and perception, in its higher, true states, *Ruach HaKodesh* provides the individual with clear, unequivocal perception, where he can actually receive information that is not otherwise available. (*See* sources at the end of this section.)

In order to understand the concept of *Ruach HaKodesh* more clearly, one must understand the precise meaning of the word *Ruach,* which is usually translated as "spirit." The meaning of this word becomes evident when we understand the Kabbalistic concept of the soul. In the Bible, we find that three words are usually used to refer to the soul, these being *Nefesh, Ruach* and *Neshamah.* According to the Kabbalists, these represent the three most important levels of the soul.

Looking at the etymology of these terms, we see that the word *Nefesh* (נֶפֶשׁ) comes from the root *Nafash,* meaning "to rest," as in the verse, "And on the seventh day, He ceased work and rested *(Nafash)" (Exodus 31:17).*

The word *Ruach* is often translated as "Spirit," but in many other places, this same word also means wind.

Finally, the word *Neshamah* (נְשָׁמָה), comes from *Neshimah* (נְשִׁימָה), the Hebrew word for breath.

The master Kabbalist, Rabbi Isaac Luriah (the Ari), explains that these three levels can be understood if we take a glassblower as an analogy.[29] The process begins with the breath *(Neshimah)* of the glassblower, blowing into a tube to form a vessel. This breath then travels through the tube as a wind *(Ruach)* until it reaches the vessel. The breath finally enters the vessel, forming it according to the desire of the glassblower, and there it comes to rest *(Nafash)*.

In the case of the soul, the "Blower" is God Himself. Thus, in describing the creation of man, the Bible says, "God formed man out of the dust of the earth, and He blew in his nostrils a soul *(Neshamah)* of life" *(Genesis 2:7)*.[30] The spirit known as *Ruach* is thus the "Breath of God" that enters into man's being.

Although God's influence constantly permeates man's being, like the air around us, it is not usually detectable. Air can only be felt when it is in motion, when we sense it as a wind *(Ruach)*. Similarly, God's spirit can only be detected when it moves in us, and it is for this reason that such spirit is also called *Ruach,* the same word as for wind.

This is also evident from the etymology of the word *Ruach* (רוּחַ). This word is closely related to the Hebrew word *Oreach* (אוֹרֵחַ), meaning a "visitor" or "guest," as well as the word *Orach* (אֹרַח) meaning a path. Both of these words indicate a concept that is not normally present, as well as one of motion and travel. In the same respect, wind is not a normal state of the air, but is one that comes about as a result of motion.

The word *Ruach* is even more closely related to the word *Reach* (רֵיחַ), a fragrance. Just as a fragrance can be detected even though it is not otherwise visible, so can the inspiration associated with *Ruach.*

The highest of the three levels of the soul is the *Neshamah*, which is the "Breath of God," while the lowest is the *Nefesh*, the level that rests in man. The part that connects the two is that which is called *Ruach*. Therefore, when God wishes to enlighten a person or convey a message to him, it is transmitted through the level of *Ruach*. Such a person is then said to have attained *Ruach HaKodesh*, the holy *Ruach*.

This, then, is the concept of *Ruach HaKodesh,* the enlightenment aspired to in meditation. It is referred to clearly in such Biblical verses as, "A spirit *(ruach)* is poured upon us from on high" *(Isaiah 32:15)*. This is also very closely related to prophecy, as we see from the verse, "I will pour forth My spirit *(ruach)* on all flesh, and your sons and daughters shall prophesy" *(Joel 3:1)*.

All things in the spiritual realm consist of ten levels, corresponding to the Ten Divine Emanations (*Sefirot*), discussed at great length in Kabbalistic literature. Each of the three levels of the soul therefore also contains these ten levels. Since the level of *Ruach* is higher than that of *Nefesh*, one must ascend through all the ten levels of the *Nefesh* before he reaches the *Ruach*. Therefore, in order to attain the enlightenment of *Ruach HaKodesh*, one must first purify all ten levels of the *Nefesh*.[31]

There are mehods especially prescribed for purifying these ten levels. These are the ten steps leading to *Ruach HaKodesh* outlined in the Talmud:[32]

> Study
> Carefulness
> Diligence
> Cleanliness
> Abstention
> Purity
> Piety
> Humility
> Fear of Sin
> Holiness

According to this program, one begins with constant study and observance, leading to scrupulous care not to violate any religious law. The next step is constant diligence to obey every commandment, and then to live a completely clean life, both in thought and in deed. One then reaches a level where he avoids even permissible things when they can possibly lead to wrong, and once this is accomplished, he can purify himself of all evil, past and present.

The individual is then ready to live a life of piety, dedicating himself to God far beyond the call of law, and this leads to humility, the negation of the ego. A person can then gain such a clear perception of good that he literally dreads sin, being totally aware of the banality of evil. He is then ready for the highest of these ten steps, holiness, the total negation of the physical.

The very next level is that of *Ruach HaKodesh*. These ten

steps thus provide a program of discipline for the individual who wishes to attain true enlightenment.

It is interesting to note that one of the most popular devotional texts, *Path of the Just (Mesilat Yesharim)* by Rabbi Moshe Chaim Luzzatto (1707–1747), is nothing more than a commentary on these ten levels.[33] This text is studied by individuals in all walks of life, but few realize that it was originally conceived as a handbook for initiates who sought to enter the highest realms of enlightenment. With a background in Kabbalah, however, it immediately becomes evident that the ten levels discussed in this book correspond directly to the ten levels of the *Sefirot.* What the author is actually doing then, is categorizing all the devotional teachings in the Bible, Talmud and Midrash according to these ten levels.

Although the Kabbalists provide many detailed meditations aimed at the attainment of *Ruach HaKodesh,* it is universally recognized that this level can also be attained by intense devotion and prayer. For this reason, before describing the system of meditations used to attain such enlightenment, Rabbi Chaim Vital states, "This level can also be attained through sanctification and Torah study on the part of the individual, without resorting to any other practice." [34]

This idea is not confined to the Kabbalists. It is actually based on an ancient Midrash, which states, "When a person reads the Torah, Prophets and Writings (the Bible), and spends his days in the Academy, he immediately becomes worthy of *Ruach HaKodesh.*" [35] An even older source, dating from the second century, states, "If an individual accepts upon himself even one commandment with perfect faith, he becomes worthy of *Ruach HaKodesh.*" [36]

Another important teaching regarding the enlightenment of *Ruach HaKodesh* is its universality. It is not a respector of person or place, as the Prophet Elijah taught his disciples, "I call heaven and earth to bear witness that any person, Jew or Gentile, man or woman, freeman or slave, if his deeds are worthy, then *Ruach HaKodesh* will descend upon him." [37] It is significant to note that this teaching is quoted in a number of Kabbalistic texts dealing with meditation.[38] The ultimate enlightenment of all humanity is also evident from the prophecy of Joel, who said in God's name, "I will pour out My spirit on *all flesh*" *(Joel 3:1).*

◇ ◇ ◇

SOURCES

An individual having all the necessary qualifications can delve into the mysteries *(Pardes),* advancing in these deep, subtle concepts and gaining a firm understanding and perception of them.

At the same time, he must also sanctify himself and separate himself from the ways of the masses, who grope in the darkness of the times. He must achieve constant diligence in not even thinking of nonessentials or considering the current vanities and intrigues.

Such a person must work on himself until his mind is constantly clear and directed on high. He must bind his intellect to the Throne of Glory, striving to comprehend the purity and holiness of the transcendental. He must furthermore contemplate on the wisdom of God in each thing, understanding its true significance, whether it be the highest spiritual entity or the lowliest thing on earth.

The individual who does this immediately becomes worthy of *Ruach HaKodesh.* When he attains this spirit, his soul becomes bound up on the level of the angels . . . and he becomes a completely different person. He can now understand things with a knowledge completely different than anything that he ever experienced previously. The level that he has attained is far above that of other men, who can merely use their intellect. This is the meaning of what [the prophet Samuel told] King Saul, "[The spirit of God shall descend upon you,] you shall prophesy with them, and you shall be transformed into a different man" *(1 Samuel 10:6).*

> *Rabbi Moses Maimonides (Rambam):*
> *1135–1204,*
> *Leading Philosopher and Codifier.*[39]

◇ ◇ ◇

God ordained that man should naturally be able to teach himself, understand, and reason with his intellect, and thus gain knowledge for his observation of things and their properties. On the basis of this knowledge, man is able to infer and deduce things that are not immediately apparent, and he can thus gain a more complete understanding of things. This is the natural process of human reason.

Besides this, however, God also decreed that there exist another, much higher, means of gaining knowledge. This is what we call "bestowed enlightenment."

Bestowed enlightenment consists of an influence granted by God through various means especially designated for this purpose. When such influence enters a person's mind, certain information becomes fixed in his intellect. He perceives this information clearly, without any doubt or error, understanding it completely, with all its causes and effects, as well as its place in the general scheme. This enlightenment is called *Ruach HaKodesh*.

In this manner, one can gain knowledge of things otherwise accessible to human reason, but in a much clearer manner. But at the same time, he can also gain information that could not otherwise be gained through mere logic. This includes such things as information concerning future events and hidden mysteries.

This experience can take place on many different levels. These involve the intensity of the influence, the time for which it is granted, the manner through which it reaches the individual, and the nature of what is revealed and communicated in this fashion. In every case, however, the influence comes in such a manner that the individual is clearly aware of it.

It is also possible that such influence be extended to a person's mind so that he is able to clearly perceive a given concept without being aware of this influence. In such a case, it is experienced like any other idea that spontaneously arises in one's mind. In a broader sense, this is also called *Ruach HaKodesh* or "Hidden Influence" in the words of the sages, [even though it is actually a much lower level]. To the person worth of it, however, true *Ruach HaKodesh* is a manifest experience, where one is highly aware of its influence.

There is yet another level, that is much higher than *Ruach HaKodesh*. This is the level of true prophecy.

This is a degree of inspiration in which the individual reaches a level where he literally binds himself to God in such a way that he actually feels this attachment. He then clearly

realizes that the One to whom he is bound is God. This is sensed
with complete clarity, with an awareness that leaves no room
for any doubt whatsoever. The individual is as certain of it as
he would be if it were a physical object observed with his
physical senses.

The main concept of true prophecy, then, is that a living
human being achieves such an attachment and bond with God.
This in itself is an extremely high state of perfection. Besides
this, however, it is also often accompanied by certain information and enlightenment. Through prophecy, one can gain
knowledge of many lofty truths among God's hidden mysteries.
These things are perceived very clearly, just as all knowledge
gained through bestowed enlightenment. Prophecy, however,
comes with much greater intensity than *Ruach HaKodesh*.

Rabbi Moshe Chaim Luzzatto (1707–1747),
Master Kabbalist and Philosopher.[40]

PART TWO

The Prophets

1

Spiritual Power

Many people consider the prophets of the Bible to be nothing more than spokesmen and agitators, who spoke out against the wrongs of their people and governments. What is not generally known is the fact that these prophets were among the greatest mystics of all times, actively engaged in the loftiest meditative techniques. The great spiritual power of the prophets is attested to by the force of their message, which after almost three thousand years, still influences a large segment of humanity.

One reason why the prophets are not usually recognized as mystics is because, with the possible exception of Ezekiel, they record very little of their mystical experiences. Of their techniques, only the vaguest hints are recorded in the Bible, and we must rely totally on the teachings of the Kabbalists, who preserved some traditions from the prophets. It is only in their writings that we gain insight into the fascinating world of the prophets of the Bible.

Before we begin to discuss the prophets, it would be useful to study the exact meaning of the word *Navie,* the Hebrew word for "prophet."

Some early sources state that the word *Navie* (נָבִיא) comes from the same root as the word *Niv* (נִיב), as in the verse, "He created the fruit *(Niv)* of the lips" *(Isaiah 57:19).*[1] According to this, the main connotation of the word *Navie* is indeed that of a spokesman, especially one who speaks in God's name. There are, however, other verses, where this word refers to a spokesman in general, as in the passage, "Aaron your brother shall be your prophet *(Navie)*" *(Exodus 7:1).*

In this view, the word *Nava* (נבא), meaning to prophesy, refers primarily to the verbal expression of the revelation. As such, it may be related to the word *Navach* (נבח), meaning to bark or cry out.

Others, however, dispute this opinion, and contend that the main connotation of the word *Navie* is that of a channel, through which spiritual force can flow. The eminent philologist, Rabbi Solomon Pappenheim (1750–1814), states that it is related to the root *Boa* (בּוֹא), meaning to "come" or "bring." [2] According to this, the main ability of a prophet is to bring spiritual power, channeling it where it is needed. As we shall see, this opinion is also supported by a Biblical account of one of Ezekiel's experiences.

A similar opinion is voiced by another major linguist and philosopher, Rabbi Samson Raphael Hirsch (1808–1888). In his opinion, the word *Navie* is closely related to the root *Nava* (נבע), meaning to "flow" or "gush forth," as in the case of a spring or fountain.[3] This word also has the connotation of expression and communication.[4] The prophet or *Navie* is then one who can "gush forth" with spirit, communicating with the Divine, and expressing the will of God.

Another closely related root is *Byb* (בִּיב) or *Navuv* (נָבוּב), both meaning "hollow," as in the verse, "A hollow *(navuv)* man will gain heart" *(Job 11:12).* In this context, a prophet would be one who totally hollows himself, emptying himself of all ego, so that, like an empty pipe *(Byv),* he makes himself a channel for the Divine Spirit. Such a person would then be on the level of King David, who said of himself, "My heart is hollow within me" *(Psalms 109:22).* This indicates that David had totally annihilated his ego, and the same must be true of the prophet before he can be a vessel for the Divine.[5]

Although such philological analysis is important, an even clearer picture emerges when we look at the context of the word. Here too, we see that the word *Nava,* meaning "prophesy," actually denotes more than just speaking out in God's name.

The clearest example of this occurs with regard to Ezekiel, in his vision of the Valley of Dry Bones. Before these bones were resurrected, God told the prophet, "Prophesy to the spirit, prophesy, son of man, and say to the spirit: Thus says the Lord God, 'From the four winds, come O spirit, and blow into these corpses that they should live' " *(Ezekiel 37:9).* What God is telling Ezekiel to do is not to be a spokesman or to predict the future, but to channel spiritual force into these dead bodies. So potent was this spiritual force that it literally had the power to bring the dead back to life.[6]

In this account, Ezekiel is told to prophesy three times, and in each of these cases, it is evident that his prophecy is a channeling and "bringing" of spiritual force. It is significant to note that in all three of these places, the word *Nava,* meaning to prophesy, is paralleled in the same verse by the root *Boa,* meaning to come, or bring.[7] The appearance in all three cases of these two words in the same verse is not coincidence, but a deliberate play on words, indicating that the prophet is one who *brings* spiritual forces to bear.

This interpretation clears up several very obscure passages which speak of prophecy. The very first mention of a prophet in the Bible occurs after King Abimelech had attempted to take Sarah away from Abraham, and had been warned by God in a dream not to do so. God then tells Abimelech, "Now restore the man's wife, for he is a prophet, and he will pray for you" *(Genesis 20:7).* There are many forced attempts that try to explain why this verse mentions that Abraham was a prophet, and what effect this would have on his prayer. But if we understand that the main power of a prophet is the ability to channel spiritual energy, the reason is obvious. Through his prayer, Abraham was able to channel such spiritual energy, and it was therefore likely that his prayer would be effective.

God tells Moses, "I have made you as a god to Pharaoh, and Aaron your brother will be your prophet *(Exodus 7:1).* As we have already seen, it is from this verse in particular that a number of commentators derive the interpretation that a prophet is primarily a spokesman or interpreter. But actually,

if one carefully looks at the account, one finds that it was
Moses, and not Aaron, who spoke to Pharaoh, indicating that
Aaron never acted as a spokesman in this respect. What we do
find, however, is that Aaron was the one who brought about the
first miracles. Aaron was therefore said to be Moses' prophet,
since it was he who channeled the prophetic energy necessary
to perform these miracles.

Of course, this channeling of spiritual energy could occasionally also result in a prophetic message. This, actually, is
the main difference between a prophet and other mystics.
While the experience of other mystics is indistinct and inarticulate, that of the prophet is clear and specific. One of the
mystic's greatest difficulties is describing the mystical experience because of its indefinable, incommunicable nature, where
even on the highest levels, it is nothing more than a general
sensation of spiritual power. The true prophet, on the other
hand, is able to channel this spiritual power, focusing it clearly
enough to obtain an unambiguous message or vision.

The ability to focus spiritual energy was a task that took
great discipline and many years of intensive training. The
word that the Bible uses to describe the process of seeking
prophecy is *Hit-nave* (הִתְנַבֵּא), the reflexive *(hit-pael)* sense of
the verb *Nave,* to prophesy. This literally means that the individual is "prophesying himself." The meaning of this is that he
is focusing spiritual energy into himself, trying to obtain a
clear message while in a mystical state.

Another way in which a prophet can focus spiritual power
is when he causes others to attain a prophetic experience. A
clear case of this occurs with regard to the seventy elders, when
God told Moses, "I will distill from the spirit that is on you, and
I will place it on them" *(Numbers 11:17).* A similar idea is
found in the case of King Saul's prophetic experience, where
Samuel planned for a group of his disciples to focus prophetic
energy on Saul. The scripture relates, "He came there to the
plateau and saw a band of prophets coming toward him, and a
spirit of God succeeded on him, and he prophesied among
them" *(1 Samuel 10:10).*

In the most striking such case, we actually find that people
were forced into a prophetic state against their will. David had
escaped King Saul's wrath, and had escaped to Samuel's
academy in Ramah. The Bible relates, "Saul sent messengers

to take David, but when they saw the company of prophets prophesying with Samuel standing over them, they also prophesied themselves" *(1 Samuel 19:20)*. Note that the verse states that Samuel's group was "prophesying" *(Nava)* in a direct sense, indicating that they were transmitting and focusing prophetic energy on Saul's men. This in turn caused Saul's messengers to "prophesy themselves" *(Mit-nave)*, in a reflexive sense, where they were overwhelmed by an inward-directed prophetic experience.

The account continues to relate how Saul sent three groups of messengers, and how they were all captivated in this manner. Saul himself finally went to recapture David, and he is also overcome by a spirit of prophecy in the same manner. Unless we say that the prophetic force could actually be projected and forced on another person, this entire account must be interpreted in a manner that is very far from its literal meaning.

◇ ◇ ◇

SOURCES

There are many levels of prophecy. Just as one person may have greater intelligence than another, so one prophet can be greater in prophecy than another.

All prophets, however, have one thing in common. They all see their prophecy only in a dream or vision at night, or else during the day, while in a trance. This is what the Torah means when it says, "[If there be a prophet among you, then I, God,] will make Myself known to him in a vision — I will speak to him in a dream" *(Numbers 12:6)*.

Prophecy is also a very traumatic experience. The prophet's limbs tremble, his body becomes faint, and he loses control of his stream of consciousness. All that remains in his conscious mind is a clear understanding of what he is experiencing at the time.

We thus find in the case of Abraham, "[Abraham fell into a trance,] and a great dark dread fell upon him" *(Genesis 15:12)*. Similarly, Daniel describes his vision, saying, "[I saw this great vision and I became powerless.] My appearance was destroyed, and my strength deserted me. [I heard the sound of

His words, and I fell on the ground in a trance]" *Daniel 10:8).*

When a prophet is given a message, it is given in the form of an allegory. The interpretation of the allegory, however, is immediately implanted in the prophet's mind, and he is aware of its meaning. . . .

In some instances, the Prophet divulged both the allegory and its interpretation. In others, only the interpretation was revealed. Occasionally, only the allegory was recorded, and this is true of some of the prophecies of Ezekiel and Zechariah. All the prophets, however, only prophesied by means of allegories and metaphors. . . .

Individuals seeking to attain prophecy were known as the "sons of the prophets." [8] Even though they would do everything properly, however, it was possible that the Divine Presence would descend on them, but then again, it was also possible that it would not.

A prophet sometimes experiences prophecy only for his sake alone. It then comes to broaden his outlook, increase his knowledge, and help him learn more about these elevated concepts.

At other times, a prophet may be sent to a group of people, a city, or a national government. He then comes to prepare and instruct them, or to stop them for doing evil.

Rabbi Moses Maimonides.

◇ ◇ ◇

The prophetic experience must come about through intermediaries. A human being cannot directly attach himself to God's glory, perceiving it as one sees a man standing in front of him. The perception of God involved in true prophecy must therefore come about through God's servants, whose task it is to provide such a vision.

These intermediaries then act as lenses through which the individual sees the Glory. What the prophet actually perceives, however, is the Glory itself, and not something else. The way one sees it, however, depends on the particular intermediary involved, just as what one would see through a lens would depend on the particular type of lens.

There are therefore many degrees of perception, depend-

ing on the (spiritual) Lens *(Ispaklaria)* involved. It may cause
the subject to appear far away or very close. There can furthermore be different degrees of transparency or opaqueness in
the Lens itself.

When God reveals Himself and bestows His influence, the
prophet is greatly overwhelmed. His body and all his limbs
immediately begin to tremble, and he feels as if he is being
turned inside out.

This, however, is due to the nature of the physical. It
cannot tolerate the revelation of the spiritual, and this is particularly true when this consists of the revelation of God's own
Glory. The prophet's senses cease to operate, and his mental
faculties can no longer function independently. They have all
become dependent on God and on the influx that is being
bestowed.

As a result of this attachment of the soul *(Neshamah)*, it
gains a degree of enlightenment far beyond the powers of the
normal human intellect. This enlightenment does not come to
it because of its own nature, but as a consequence of the fact
that the highest Root is bound to it. The soul therefore perceives things in a much higher manner than it could ever
attain by itself.

The power of prophecy is therefore much greater than that
of *Ruach HaKodesh,* even with respect to providing information. Prophecy can bring the highest enlightenment possible
for man, namely that which is an aspect of his being bound to
his Creator.

The revelation of God's Glory is what initiates everything
transmitted in a prophetic vision. This is then transmitted to the imaginative faculty in the prophet's soul *(Nefesh)*,
which in turn forms images of the concepts impelled upon it by
the power of the highest revelation. The imagination, however,
does not initiate anything on its own.

These images, in turn, convey to the prophet certain ideas
and information, whose conception comes from the power of the
revealed Glory. The subject remains fixed on the prophet's
mind, and when he returns to his normal state, this knowledge
is retained with perfect clarity. . . .

When one attains a full level of prophecy, everything
comes to him with clear perception and full knowledge. This is
transmitted to him through the steps outlined, where it is first

conceived in the form of images and then translated into ideas. When an individual understands his prophecy clearly, he also becomes aware that he is truly a prophet.

He is then totally aware of the fact that he was bound to God, and that it was God Himself who was revealed to him, acting upon him in this manner. He realizes that the images that he conceived were prophetic visions, resulting from this influence of God. Knowledge of its subject matter is permanently fixed in his mind through his influence. The prophet then has no uncertainty about his being a prophet, about any aspect of his prophecy, or about its origin and results.

Rabbi Moshe Chaim Luzzatto.[10]

2

Ezekiel's Vision

In very few places do the prophets provide us with any insight
into their experiences, so that we should be able to understand
exactly what prophecy entails. One of the most fascinating
exceptions is the vision of Ezekiel, where such richness of
detail is provided as to make analysis difficult. The vision of
Ezekiel has been subject to many interpretations, but the
clearest explanation is to be found within the teachings of the
classical Kabbalistic schools.

In general, the prophet is gazing at four levels. The most
prominent is that of the *Chayot* (singular *Chayah*), a "Living"
angelic being. The *Chayot* are later identified as being the
same as the Cherubs, as the prophet says, "The Cherubs
mounted up — this is the *Chayah* that I saw by the river
Chabar" *(Ezekiel 10:5)*. The Chabar, of course, is the place
where Ezekiel had his original great vision.

Below the level of the *Chayot*, the prophet saw the
Ophanim (singular, *Ophan*), a wheel-like angelic creature.
Ezekiel thus says, "As I beheld the *Chayot,* and behold, there
was one *Ophan* on the earth, close to the *Chayot*" *(Ezekiel 1:15)*.

The prophet then sees a firmament over the heads of the

Chayot. He then gazes even higher, and describes what he sees: "Above the firmament that was over their heads was the likeness of a Throne . . . and on the likeness of the Throne was the likeness of the appearance of a Man upon it from above" *(Ezekiel 1:26).* Here we have the next two levels, first that of the Throne, and then that of the "Man" upon the Throne.

The Kabbalists explain that Ezekiel had envisioned the four supernal Universes. In Kabbalistic literature, these Universes are discussed in great detail, and are said to correspond to the four letters of the Tetragrammaton. The names of these Universes are *Atzilut* (Closeness), *Beriyah* (Creation), *Yetzirah* (Formation), and *Asiyah* (Making). They are alluded to in the verse, "All that is called by My Name, for My Glory *(Atzilut),* I have created it *(Beriyah),* I have formed it *(Yetzirah),* and I have made it *(Asiyah)*" *(Isaiah 43:7).* [11]

The highest of these four universes is called *Atzilut,* which in this verse is called "My Glory." This is the Universe of the Ten *Sefirot,* the Divine Emanations, and in Ezekiel's vision, this is represented by the "Man" on the Throne.

In order to understand this, we must keep in mind that in many places, the Bible speaks of God as if He had a body. We find such anthropomorphisms as "God's hand," and "God's eye" many places in the scripture. At first thought, this is somewhat difficult to understand, since it is well established that God is absolutely incorporeal, having neither body, shape, nor form.

An ancient Midrash resolves this, by teaching that "God borrows terms from His creatures to express His relationship with the world." [12] Still, we are not given any hint as to what the various anthropomorphic terms represent. In the Kabbalah, however, the various parts of the Divine "Body" are said to represent the various Sefirot. One of the clearest expressions of this is to be found in Elijah's introduction to the *Tikuney Zohar,* where he says:

> Love is the right hand,
> > Power is the left,
> Glory is the body,
> > Victory and Splendor are the two feet . . .
> Wisdom is the brain,
> > Understanding is the heart . . .
> And the Crown of all
> > Is the Place where *Tefillin* rests. . . .

Elijah, of course, is referring to the Sefirot. The lowest seven of these Sefirot are alluded to in the verse, "Yours, O God, are the Greatness *(Gedulah* or Love, *Chesed),* the Power *(Gevurah),* and the Glory *(Tiferet),* the Victory *(Netzach)* and the Splendor *(Hod),* for All that is in heaven and in earth *(Yesod),* Yours, O God, is the Kingdom *(Malkhut)" (1 Chronicles 29:11).*[13] Since these represent the various parts of the Divine "Body," Ezekiel saw them as a "Man" on the Throne.

The next universe is *Beriyah,* the Universe of Creation, which is also known as the Universe of the Throne. This is represented by the Throne in Ezekiel's vision. Since he sees this Throne "above the firmament that is above the heads" of the *Chayot,* "it is obvious that the Universe of the Throne is higher than that of the angels.

In general, the concept of "sitting" is that of lowering, and therefore, when we say that God "sits," we allegorically are referring to the fact that He "lowers" Himself to be concerned with the world.[14] The Throne is where God "sits," and therefore, it is the vehicle of this "lowering" and concern, which is the sum total of the Forces involved in His providence.[15]

The part of the human soul that reaches the level of *Beriyah* is that of the *Neshamah.* This highest level of the soul is the "breath of God," and represents the first stage of God's "lowering" Himself to create man and be concerned with his destiny.

The next level is *Yetzirah,* the Universe of Formation, which is the world of the angels. The angels are seen primarily as messengers, and therefore, this universe is seen as a link between God's providence and the world below.

The level of *Yetzirah* corresponds to the level of *Ruach* in the human soul, and in the soul, this is also the level that implies communication. It is for this reason that prophecy is often said to come through the means of the angels.[16] Since Ezekiel is seeing his vision on the level of *Ruach,* he appears to be standing in the world of the *Chayot.*

Finally, there is *Asiyah,* the Universe of Making, which includes the physical world and its spiritual counterpart. The angels of *Asiyah* are the *Ophanim* or "Wheels," and these are the *Ophanim* that Ezekiel saw under the *Chayot.* In the human soul, *Asiyah* corresponds to the level of *Nefesh,* which is where the spiritual actually interacts with the physical.

According to the Kabbalists, Ezekiel himself reached the level of *Yetzirah,* and this was the vantage point of his vision. It is for this reason that he relates that he "saw" the *Chayot,* since these are the angels that inhabit *Yetzirah.*

The Throne, however, was in the Universe above that in which Ezekiel had his vantage point, and this was only seen as a reflection in *Yetzirah.* The prophet therefore says that he saw "the *likeness* of a throne." Finally, the "Man on the Throne" is seen two levels above him, and this is envisioned as a reflection of a reflection. This is therefore described as "a *likeness* of the *appearance* of a Man." [17]

A close examination of Ezekiel's vision thus shows that a great deal of the structure of the Kabbalistic system is derived from it. This, however, is not the primary subject of our discussion. Much more important is the Talmudic tradition that Ezekiel's vision contains the key to the entire prophetic method. In the language of the Talmud, this is called *Maaseh Merkava,* or the "Workings of the Chariot." [18]

The term itself, used in relation to Ezekiel's vision, bears some examination. Actually, the term *Merkava* or Chariot occurs nowhere in the entire book of Ezekiel, and some find the use of this term very puzzling. At first thought, there does not seem to be any connection between this vision and any sort of "Chariot."

One place in the Bible where this word is found in such a context is in the verse, "Gold for the pattern of the Chariot (*Merkava*), the Cherubs" (*1 Chronicles 28:18*). The scripture here uses the word *Merkava* specifically to describe the Cherubs on the Ark. But, as we have seen, Ezekiel identifies the Cherubs with the *Chayot* seen in his initial vision. Therefore, the concept of the Chariot indeed does relate to his vision.[19]

The word *Merkava* (מֶרְכָּבָה) comes from the root *Rakhav* (רכב). The relationship between the Cherubs and the Chariot is therefore related to the concept expressed in the verse, "[God] *rode* on a Cherub and flew, and He swooped down on wings of spirit" (*Psalm 18:11*). It is significant to note that the root of the word Cherub (כְּרוּב) and the word Rakhav (רכב), meaning "to ride," have exactly the same letters.

In general, the concept of riding is that of traveling and leaving one's natural place. When the Bible says that God "rides," it means that he leaves His natural state where He is absolutely unknowable and inconceivable, and allows Himself to be visualized by the prophets. He is said to "swoop with wings of spirit *(Ruach)*." The term "wings" alludes to coverings, meaning that God covers and conceals His glory, not revealing it completely, since if He did so, the prophet would be overwhelmed and blinded. The spiritual force through which the vision is granted is *Ruach,* related to *Ruach HaKodesh,* discussed in the previous section.

The word *Merkava* comes from the root *Rakhav,* "to ride," and hence refers to a "riding vehicle." In general, then, it refers to the complete system and mechanism through which God "leaves His place" and reveals himself to those who are worthy.

The idea of *Maaseh Merkava* or "Workings of the Merkava" refers to the setting up of a *Merkava,* that is, placing oneself in a state where he can attain a *Merkava* vision. From the context in which this term is used in the Kabbalah texts, it is obvious that *Maaseh Merkava* refers to the meditative techniques involved in attaining this mystical experience. For example, one very early test speaks of the individual making a "Chariot of Light," through which he ascends to the supernal worlds.[20]

The Talmudic tradition therefore teaches that the vision of Ezekiel contains at least an allusion to the mystical techniques of the prophets. Although the entire vision requires study, the most important part may be its opening verse, which is often ignored. The prophet says, "I looked, and behold, a stormy wind coming from the north, a great cloud and flashing fire, and a glow round about it, and from its midst, the vision of the *Chashmal,* in the midst of the fire" *(Ezekiel 1:4)*. In the next section, the significance of the "glow" and the *Chashmal* will be discussed in relation to two types of meditation used by the prophet. But in general, this verse requires study, since it shows how the prophet actually enters into his mystical state.

The *Zohar* teaches that the "stormy wind," the "great cloud," and the "flashing fire" refer to the three levels of the *Klipah,* the "Husk" that is the root of all evil.[21] These confuse the mind, and serve as barriers to one who would ascend into the spiritual domain. According to the *Zohar,* they also correspond to the three barriers visualized by Elijah: "A great strong wind . . . an earthquake . . . and a fire . . . and after the fire, a

still small voice" *(1 Kings 19:11, 12)*. In both cases, the prophet
is speaking of levels of experience that precede true prophecy,
but in the case of Elijah, the scripture is more explicit in stating
that one follows the other.

In the vision of Ezekiel, we see the prophetic experience
beginning with great agitation, visualized as a "stormy wind."
Literally, this is a "stormy *Ruach*" *(Ruach Sa'arah)*, and
hence, it can also be translated as a "stormy spirit." These are
the natural agitations of the mind, which become greatly ex-
aggerated when a person reaches a high meditative state. In
the absolute calm of his meditation, the mind becomes highly
sensitive, and the slightest extraneous thought is like an
earthquake, a tornado, disturbing this calm. This is the first
barrier through which the prophet must pass.[22]

The prophet then encounters a "great cloud." This is an
opaqueness of the mind, where nothing can be seen or experienced, and it will discourage the prophet if he does not have the
will to proceed further. The prophet tries to ascend to higher
levels, but he finds himself facing a barrier, beyond which he
cannot see. He must work and strive to penetrate this cloud,
which is the second *Klipah*.

Since Elijah's prophetic experience was audial, rather
than visual like that of Ezekiel, he describes the second barrier
as a "loud noise," a *Ra'ash,* in Hebrew. Although often translated as an "earthquake," in this context it is more like an
undifferentiated white noise, in which no coherent sound can
be discerned. As such, it is the audial equivalent of an opaque
cloud.

The third thing the prophet experienced was awe, shame,
and dread, this being exemplified by fire. While the cloud is an
obliteration of sensation, the fire is an overabundance of sensation, which threatens and repels the prophet. The cloud shows
the prophet that one who is not worthy will see nothing, while
the fire indicates that there can be great danger as well.

The prophet entering into the mystical experience first
experiences strong agitation, then a stifling lack of sensation,
and finally, a burning overabundance of sensation. He must
then continue to rise spiritually until he reaches the level of
the *Nogah,* the "glow." From the context in which the word is
generally used, it refers to light shining out of darkness, and it
is in this sense that the word *Nogah* is also used to denote dawn

and twilight. What the prophet must do is blank out all of these sensations of storm, cloud and fire, which are aspects of the *Klipah* and spiritual darkness, and concentrate on the light that shines out from this darkness.

When the prophet reaches this level, his ego is totally nullified and all sensation is hushed. He then reaches the level of the *Chashmal,* which is identical with the "small still voice" of Elijah. The Talmud states that the word *Chashmal* is made up of two words, *Chash,* meaning silence, and *Mal,* indicating speech. At this level, the prophet experiences the "speaking silence." This is the level of silence through which he can hear the word of God or see a true divine vision.

The Bible then goes on to describe the entire vision of Ezekiel, including the levels of the *Chayot,* the Throne, and the Man on the Throne. All of these are elements of the Chariot, the system through which God reveals Himself and controls the reins of creation. Only after visualizing the entire structure is the prophet able to focus his vision clearly enough to hear a prophetic message. The entire account ends, "I fell on my face and I heard a voice speaking" *(Ezekiel 1:28).* As the commentaries note, all of the prophets actually visualized the entire *Merkava* before hearing a word, but Ezekiel was the only one who described it explicitly.[23]

The renowned philosopher and Kabbalist, Rabbi Moses ben Nachman (Ramban: 1194–1270) notes that the account of the *Merkava* occurring in the Book of Ezekiel "contains the Names which are the keys to the supernal Chambers." [24] One gets a very strong impression that certain parts of this account were repeated, very much like a mantra, in order to bring a person to the mystical state. A number of Kabbalists say this explicitly with regard to the first verse of Ezekiel, "In the thirtieth year, in the fourth month, on the fifth day of the month, as I was among the captives by the river Chabar, that the heavens were opened and I saw the visions of God" *(Ezekiel 1:1).* The Kabbalists note that in the original Hebrew, this verse contains 72 letters.[25] This would then be very much like the Name of 72 letters, which is often discussed as a mantra-like device, especially in the writings of Rabbi Abraham Abulafia (1240–1300).[26] From the words of these Kabbalists, it appears that this entire verse can be used as a mantra-like device, where one repeats it over and over, until the "heavens are opened."

In most editions of the Bible, however, this verse does not contain 72 letters, but 74. This is due to the fact that some minor spelling variations are found in the Bible, especially in the later books of the Prophets. What makes this very significant is the fact that the fourth verse, "And I looked, and behold, a stormy wind coming from the north . . ." has precisely 73 letters. With a minor variation in spelling, however, this verse could also have 72 letters. It would therefore be interesting to conjecture that this verse might also have been used as a meditative device, for those who wished to ascend to a level above the mere "opening of the heaven." Indeed, this may have been part of the discipline involved in the *Maaseh Merkavah.*

A third verse which comes very close to having 72 letters is the passage, "And above the firmament that was over their heads was the likeness of a Throne . . ." (Ezekiel 1:26). This verse has 71 letters, but again, with a slight spelling adjustment, it could also have 72. This could then be used for a device to visualize the higher levels of *Beriyah* and *Atzilut.*

There are three verses in the Book of Exodus (14:19–21), which also have exactly 72 letters each. It is out of these three verses that the Name of Seventy-two is derived, and this plays an important role in all Kabbalah meditation.[27] What is a very interesting possibility is that these three verses from Ezekiel might also be used in a similar manner.

In any event, classical Kabbalah literature is silent regarding the use of these verses, and it does not tell us anything about the use of the account of Ezekiel's vision for mystical purposes in any manner. All that we have is conjecture, interesting though it may be. But besides this, there is actually a considerable literature describing how a prophetic state can be attained.

THE THREE VERSES FROM EZEKIEL
CONTAINING 72 LETTERS EACH

וַיְהִי בִּשְׁלֹשִׁים שָׁנָה בָּרְבִיעִי בַּחֲמִשָּׁה לַחֹדֶשׁ וַאֲנִי בְתוֹךְ־
הַגּוֹלָה עַל־נְהַר כְּבָר נִפְתְּחוּ הַשָּׁמַיִם וָאֶרְאֶה מַרְאוֹת
אֱלֹהִים:

And it was in the thirtieth year, in the fourth month, on
the fifth day of the month, as I was among the captives by
the river Chabar, the heavens were opened and I saw the
visions of God. (1:1)

וָאֵרֶא וְהִנֵּה רוּחַ סְעָרָה בָּאָה מִן־הַצָּפוֹן עָנָן גָּדוֹל וְאֵשׁ
מִתְלַקַּחַת וְנֹגַהּ לוֹ סָבִיב וּמִתּוֹכָהּ כְּעֵין הַחַשְׁמַל
מִתּוֹךְ הָאֵשׁ:

And I looked, and behold, a stormy wind coming from the
north, a great cloud and flashing fire, and a glow round
about it, and from its midst, the vision of the Chashmal, in
the midst of the fire. (1:4)

וּמִמַּעַל לָרָקִיעַ אֲשֶׁר עַל־רֹאשָׁם כְּמַרְאֵה אֶבֶן־סַפִּיר
דְּמוּת כִּסֵּא וְעַל דְּמוּת הַכִּסֵּא דְּמוּת כְּמַרְאֵה אָדָם עָלָיו
מִלְמָעְלָה:

And above the firmament that was over their heads, like a
vision of sapphire, there was the form of a Throne, and
above the form of the Throne, was a form like the vision of a
man on it from above. (1:26)

◇ ◇ ◇

SOURCES

Ezekiel's Vision

And it was in the thirtieth year, in the fourth month, on the fifth of the month, while I was among the exiles on the river Chebar, and the heavens were opened, and I saw visions of God.

(On the fifth of the month, in the fifth year of the exile of King Yehoiachin, the word of God had come to Ezekiel ben Buzi, in the land of the Chaldeans, on the river Chebar, and the hand of God was upon him.)

I saw, and behold a stormy wind *(ruach)* come from the north, a great cloud and flashing fire, and a Glow *(nogah)* round about, and from its midst a vision of the Speaking Silence *(Chashmal),* in the midst of the fire.

And from its midst was the form of four Chayot (Living Creatures) — this was their form — they had a human form. Each one had four faces and every one had four wings. Their feet were straight, and the soles of their feet were like those of a calf's foot, and they shined like a vision of polished copper.

Human hands were under their wings on all four sides, and all four had faces and wings. Their wings were joined to each other, and they did not turn when they went. Each one moved in the direction of their faces as they went.

The form of their faces were the face of a man, with the face of a lion to the right of the four, the face of an ox to the left of the four, and the face of an eagle to the four. Their faces and wings were separated on top. For each one, two connected the individuals, and two covered their bodies. Each individual moved in the direction of his face. They went to where the *Ruach*-spirit was to go. They did not turn as they went.

The form of the Chayot had the appearance of burning coals of fire. Walking between the Chayot was a vision of torches, and a Glow *(nogah)* for fire, and from the fire went forth sparks.

The Chayot ran and returned, like a vision of lightning.

Then I gazed at the Chayot, and behold, there was a single Ophan (Wheel) on the earth near the Chayot. [One was] on each of its four faces.

The appearance of the Ophanim and their actions was like a vision of Topaz. All four had a single form, and their appearance and actions were as if there was an Ophan within an Ophan.

They moved on their four sides as they went — they did not turn as they went. They had high backs and were filled with fear. The backs of all four were filled with eyes.

When the Chayot moved, the Ophanim went near them. When the Chayot rose up from the earth, the Ophanim were also lifted. Where the *ruach*-spirit had to go, there the *ruach*-spirit of the Chayah was in the Ophanim. When one went, so went the other; when one stood, so stood the other. And when they were lifted from the earth, the Ophanim were lifted beside them, for the *ruach*-spirit of Chayah was in the Ophanim.

The form above the heads of the Chayah was that of a firmament, looking like a fearsome ice, spread out above their heads. Under the firmament, their wings were straight out, one towards another. For each individual, two covered them, and for each individual, two covered their bodies.

Then I heard the sound of their wings, like the sound of many waters, like the voice of the Almighty *(Shaddai)* when they went. The sound of their tumult was like the sound of an armed camp — when they stood still, they let down their wings. And there was a sound from the firmament which was above their heads — when they stood still, they let down their wings.

Above the firmament that was over their heads, like a vision of a sapphire, was the form of a Throne, and over the form of the Throne, there was a form like a vision of a Man, on it from above.

And I saw a vision of the Speaking Silence *(Chashmal)* like a vision of fire, as a house for it round about, from the vision of His thighs and above. And from the vision of His thighs and below, I saw a vision like fire, with a Glow *(nogah)* around it. Like a vision of the rainbow in the clouds on a rainy day, so was the vision of the Glow around. This was the vision of God's Glory. I saw it, and I fell on my face. Then I heard a voice speak.

It said to me, "Son of man, stand up on your feet, and I will speak to you." Then a *ruach*-spirit came in me, and it spoke to me. It stood me on my feet, and I heard that which spoke to me.

Ezekiel 1:1–2:2.

◇ ◇ ◇

Elijah's Vision

[Elijah] came there to a cave, and he spent the night there. God's word then came to him, and it said to him, "What are you doing here, Elijah?"

He replied, "I have been very zealous for the Lord, God of Hosts, for the children of Israel have abandoned Your covenant, they have overthrown Your altars, and they have killed Your prophets with the sword. I alone remain, and they seek to take my life."

[God] had said to him, "Go out, and stand on the mountain before God." God then passed by.

There was a great strong wind, sundering mountains and smashing bedrock, before God. But God was not in the wind.

After the wind came a great noise. But God was not in the noise.

After the noise, there was a fire. But God was not in the fire.

Then, after the fire, there was a still soft voice.

When Elijah heard this, he wrapped his face in his mantle and went out. He stood by the entrance of the cave, and the voice came to him and said, "What are you doing here, Elijah?"

He replied, "I have been very zealous for the Lord, God of Hosts, for the children of Israel have abandoned Your covenant, they have overthrown Your altars, and they have killed Your prophets with the sword. I alone remain, and they seek to take my life."

1 Kings 19:9–14.

◇ ◇ ◇

Some authorities interpret these verses as revealing the essence of prophecy. . . .

The "stormy wind" alludes to the ecstasy of the prophet when he begins to experience prophecy. His faculties become very agitated with great ecstasy so that he is overcome with great trembling, as if a powerful wind was blowing and a tornado was throwing him about. Daniel was referring to such an experience when he said, "My appearance was obliterated, and my strength deserted me" *(Daniel 10:8)*. Eliphaz likewise said, "Then a spirit (wind, *ruach*) passed before my face, and it made the hair of my flesh stand on end" *(Job 4:15)*. Ezekiel himself, when prophecy came upon him, had said, "A spirit (wind, *ruach*) lifted me, and behind me, I heard a great voice" *(Ezekiel 3:12)*.

This then is also the meaning of the verse, "Behold a stormy wind (spirit, *ruach*) came from the north." The verse mentions a north wind in particular, since the north wind is known to be very strong. It is thus written, "The north wind brings forth rain" *(Proverbs 25:23)*. Therefore, in order to indicate the strength of this wind, the Bible says that it came from the north.

The great cloud that Ezekiel saw alludes to his ignorance of the future. He thus sees it as if "a fearsome darkness fell on him" *(Genesis 15:12)*. A cloud surrounds him since he does not know what the end will be.

The "flashing fire" alludes to the influx of prophecy that reaches his mind, which in its power, is like purifying fire. This is what God told Jeremiah, "Are not my words like fire?" *(Jeremiah 23:29)*. Jeremiah himself also said, "It was in my heart like burning fire" *(Jeremiah 20:9)*.

Rabbi Isaac Abarbanel (1437–1508),
Commentator and Philosopher.[28]

◇ ◇ ◇

An excerpt from
THE GATES OF HOLINESS

It is taught that there is a single Light, in the form of a Man, which radiates through all the four Universes, *Atzilut, Beriyah, Yetzirah* and *Asiyah,* reaching down to the physical elements. This Light is bound to the Lights of the Supernal Man, which are called the Ten *Sefirot*. These are clothed in this Light, which is called the "Light of the Quarry of Souls," and in it are included all souls below.

These souls descend to the physical world, clothing themselves in physical bodies. Their roots, however, remain attached to their source, from which they were hewn, and only the branches of these roots descend. They do so by reaching down and clothing themselves in physical bodies in the physical world.

The case resembles branches of a tree. The branches are attached to the trunk of a tree, but when they are bent over, they can touch the ground, even though they are still attached to the tree trunk.

When a person commits a sin for which the punishment is being "cut off" *(Korait),* the branch is cut off from the body of the tree. It then remains separated, and remains in the physical world like the spirit of any other animal. This is the deeper meaning of the verse, "That soul shall be cut off . . ." *(Numbers 15:31).*

This is also the inner meaning of the verse, "Man is a tree of the field" *(Deuteronomy 20:19).* It is also the mystical reason why the names of some saints are doubled in the Bible, as "Abraham, Abraham" *(Genesis 22:11),* "Jacob, Jacob" *(Genesis 46:2),* and "Moses Moses" *(Exodus 3:4).* The first name corresponds to the Root that remains on high, attached to the Tree, [while the second name is the branch that rests in the physical world].

This [Root] is also referred to as a person's *Mazal* (Destiny). The sages teach that Moses saw the *Mazal* of Rabbi Akiba, sitting [and teaching.[29] The word *Mazal* (מַזָּל) comes from the root *Nazal* (נזל), meaning "to flow downward."] This is because spiritual sustenance *(Shefa)* flows downward [from the *Mazal*] to the branch which has descended and clothed itself in a physical body.

This Root is very high, originating at the very top of the Universe of *Atzilut.* The branch is very long, descending through all the universes until its lower end is clothed in the physical body.

In each level, in every Universe, this branch leaves a root. Therefore, there is no soul that does not have an infinite number of roots, one above the other. Through a person's deeds, he can be worthy of elevating them all.

All the roots that are left on all the levels of the Universe of *Asiyah* together are called "a complete soul *(Nefesh)* of *Asiyah.*" The same is true of the other levels.

This explains the concept of prophecy. The individual

must be in a pure state, not tainted by the Evil Urge, and beyond the grasp of everything pertaining to the physical. He must be completely free of any sin that would blemish any of the roots of his soul. Only then, if he prepares himself properly, can he attach himself to the highest Root.

Even though an individual is worthy for it, however, he must still divest his soul from all mundane things, separating it from all physical concepts. Only then can it be attached to its spiritual Root.

The is the concept of "divestment," discussed in all the texts with regard to *Ruach HaKodesh* and Prophecy. It does not refer to actual divestment, where the soul would actually leave the body, as when one sleeps. If this were the case, the person would not experience prophecy, but it would be like any other dream. But *Ruach HaKodesh* is experienced when the individual's soul is in his body, when he is awake, and when his soul has not left him.

The true concept of divestment is that one must banish all thought completely. The power of speech, which is the faculty derived from the living soul which pertains to the physical elements, must cease to imagine, to think, or to contemplate any thought dealing with the mundane world, just as if the soul had actually left him.

The faculty of the imagination in the individual's consciousness is then reversed. It imagines and depicts as if it were ascending to the supernal Universes, through the roots of the soul that are in each one. The consciousness rises from one to the other, until the depiction of the imagination reaches his highest Root.

The form of all the Lights become engraved in the individual's mind, just as if he had actually visualized them and seen them. It is very much like the faculty of imagination can depict physical concepts in the mind, even though they are not seen, as known to psychology.

The individual must then concentrate his thoughts so as to receive Light from the Ten Sefirot, from the point where the Root of his soul is attached to them.

First, he must concentrate so as to elevate the Ten Sefirot, each one to the one above it, until he reaches the Infinite Being (*Ain Sof*). He then draws illumination downward to them, to the very lowest level.[30]

Through this individual, then, Light descends to the

Sefirot and they rejoice. They then radiate with the Light transmitted to them to the Root of the individual's soul where it is bound to them, in a measure appropriate for it.

The individual must then concentrate his thoughts to bring down the Light of that influx from level to level, until it reaches the Intelligent Soul in his body. From there it reaches his Vital Soul and its faculty of imagination. Here, these concepts are depicted as a physical image through the imaginative faculty. The individual then understands them, as if he had literally seen them with his eyes.

Sometimes, the Light that descends is depicted in the individual's imaginative faculty in the form of an angel speaking to him. He sees it or hears its voice, sensing it with one of the five [spiritual] senses in his imaginative faculty.

From this level, it is transferred to its external aspect. This appears in the five external senses, which are also in the Vital Soul, as is well known. The individual then sees, hears, smells, and speaks literally, with his physical senses. Regarding this, it is written, "The spirit *(Ruach)* of God spoke in me, and His word was on my tongue" *(2 Samuel 23:2)*. The Light thus becomes physical so that it can be detected with the physical senses. Sometimes, however, a prophecy is only detected by the five spiritual senses in the imaginative faculty.

All this takes place when the imaginative faculty is completely divested of all mundane thoughts, as discussed earlier.

Prophecy is therefore seen as a dream. The Intelligent Soul leaves the individual and ascends step by step, and there it perceives and sees. It then goes back and descends, infusing this Light into the Vital Soul, which is the imaginative faculty. There, these things are depicted in an even more physical sense.

When the individual awakens, his soul remembers these things through the grasping faculty and the faculty of memory. These are also in the Vital Soul, as known to psychology.[31]

This explains the concept of prophecy and that of dreams. One occurs while the soul remains in the individual's body, and one when the soul is absent.

In prophecy itself, however, there are two categories.

The first is the prophecy of all prophets [other than Moses]. In its descent, the Light that is bestowed reaches the individual's Intellectual Soul. From there, it descends to the

Vital Soul, where it is depicted in the imaginative faculty, in the five internal senses. The external senses are then agitated, and the prophet is overcome with great trembling. Since he does not have the strength to accept the Light, he would fall to the ground. When they try to imagine this Light and perceive it with their physical senses, they are simply overwhelmed.

Even though it is very different from a normal dream, prophecy such as this is often referred to as a "dream." Regarding this type of prophecy it is thus written, "A trance fell on Abraham, [and a great dark dread fell upon him]" *(Genesis 15:12)*.

The second type of prophecy is perfect. Here, the physical senses are not agitated at all, and all things are perceived with perfect serenity. This was the level of the prophecy of Moses.[32]

The reason for this was that his physical being was also spiritually transparent. As a result of his deeds, it was altered until it was on the same level as the soul. All taint of sin had been removed, and only the good and the pure remained in his body. This was also true of that which pertains to the physical elements, for this had been raised to the level of the intellect.

It has already been discussed how man's soul has countless Roots. The higher the source of these Roots, the greater will be their power to transmit the influx of prophecy. But even if the source of the Root of one's soul is on a very high level, unless he rectifies it and purifies it so that it transmits to all the Roots that are below it, he cannot transmit the prophetic influx. The only levels from which he can transmit it are those which he is worthy of because he has rectified them, and from there alone will his prophetic influx be transmitted. This explains why there are countless levels among prophets.

We have explained that the soul of the prophet does not leave his body. Do not think however, that when he ascends to open the gates, this has no actual substance, and exists only in his thoughts. Actually, however, this can be understood through that which was mentioned earlier, that the soul is like a very long branch, with its Root attached to the Tree, and reaching to man's physical body. When man yearns to ascend to this Root, the soul becomes like a transmission line, bringing information from the Root.

The Light of the individual's thought is called the Concept *(Muskal –* מֻשְׂכָּל *).* This Light ascends through the enlightened soul of this individual, who is the "thinker" (*Maskil* – מַשְׂכִּיל). It ascends to the level of Pure Thought (*Sekhel* – שֵׂכֶל), which is the highest Root of his soul. The three [concept, thinker, and thought] are bound together, and become one through the process of Enlightenment (*Haskalah* – הַשְׂכָּלָה). This is the influx transmitted from Pure Thought to the thinker.

The Concept *(Muskal)* is thus the light and flow itself, descending from Pure Thought *(Sekhel)* to the enlightened soul. This influx and light is the concept that is called "thought" *(Machashava)*.

Understand this well, for it is not an empty teaching. Were it not true, all the concepts of special intents in prayer, as well as human thought, whether good or bad, would no longer exist.

This explains why prophecy is both possible and necessary. The process is very much like that of a person grasping one end of a branch with his hand, and shaking it with all his strength. The entire tree must then also shake.

The highest entities, however, do not vibrate because of the thoughts of a physical human being unless he is worthy of transmitting the highest Lights to them. If he does not have this power, they ignore him completely. In such a case, they do not desire to bring themselves close to him, or to help him and draw his thoughts on high. All of his efforts will then be vain and useless.

        ·   ·   ·   ·

It has already been explained that there are four universes, *Atzilut, Beriyah, Yetzirah,* and *Asiyah.* Below them is the physical world, consisting of the elements. The elements and their spiritual counterparts are divided just like the Ten Sefirot.

It has also been explained that in each Universe, there is an Inner Light *(Or Penimi),* this being the Light of the Ten Sefirot. Outside of this is the Light of the Quarry of Souls, and outside that, the Light of the Quarry of Angels. Outside of these is the Darkening Light, the Quarry of the Husks *(Klipot).* Finally, outside them all is the Universe itself. [The division between the substance of each Universe and the Lights that are in it] is the "firmament" of each Universe.

The same is literally true of the physical world. The

human body and the universe itself consist of the substance of the elements. Inside it are the other Lights, each one consisting of the concepts included in the Elemental Soul.

It has also been explained that there are countless levels. Each of the Ten Sefirot contains ten levels, and each of these in turn also consists of ten. Each universe therefore has an infinite number of levels.

The concept of prophecy has also been discussed. The thought of the prophet is divested from his body and ascends upward, from level to level, until it reaches the place where the Root of his soul is attached [to the Sefirot]. He then concentrates to elevate the Light of the Sefirot to the Infinite Being *(Ain Sof)*, and from there transmit Light [to the Sefirot].

The prophet then descends through the same steps through which he ascended, until he returns to the level of his Intellectual Soul. He takes his portion of the Light according to the degree of the grasp of his soul Root on high. From there he transmits it, through his imaginative faculty, in his Vital Soul. These Lights are then depicted with the internal senses in the imaginative faculty, as well as with the external senses.

It is important to understand how thought is transmitted on high. It obviously does not ascend automatically. The prophet must make use of meditations *(Kavanot)* and Unifications *(Yechudim)*, given over to him by the [master] prophet, who teaches him the methods of prophecy. [Such disciples] are called the "sons of the prophets," who were with Samuel, Elijah and Elisha.

Through such Unifications, one can transmit Light and Influx as he desires. This is the ultimate concept of prophecy.

The master prophets also taught another discipline. This consisted of prayers and the utterance of Divine Names, whispered to the [angels who] guard the gates of the firmaments and the chambers of each Universe.[33] Through these, the prophets ascend through each of the four Universes, and through the space between them, until they reach the highest, which is *Atzilut*.

At first they would work to open the gates of a particular level. Then they would meditate on the Unification and recite the particular prayer appropriate to that level. In this manner, they would ascend from level to level, until they reached their highest Root, and there they would stand. Then, they would

transmit their thoughts up to the Infinite Being *(Ain Sof)*, and
finally, they would return, transmitting the influx down
below.

This is the concept of the Gates and Names. The power of
each Name is derived from the Sefirah that is on that particular level. The prophet would utter it to the angel who is rooted
and quarried from there, binding the angel by an oath. Such an
angel is the overseer of the gate of the gate of the firmament of
that level, this being the substance of the level.

When the prophet would make use of the Name specific for
that gate, the angel would open it. The mind of the prophet
would then enter through that gate, ascending from Light to
Light, until he would reach the innermost Light of the Sefirot
on that level. He would then recite the necessary prayer and
meditate on the required Unification. It was in this manner
that he would ascend step by step.

The vision of Ezekiel is called the "Workings of the
Chariot" or Vehicle. This is because each level is a vehicle for
the next.

At the beginning of this vision, "the heavens were opened"
(Ezekiel 1:1). This refers to the gates of the firmaments, which
are the Lights consisting of the substance and the vessels of
that Universe.

From there, the prophet entered the realm of the Husks
(Klipot). Regarding this, he said, "I saw, and behold, a stormy
wind came from the north, great cloud and flashing fire"
(Ezekiel 1:4).

The same idea is found in the case of the prophet Hosea.
The book begins with the words, "The beginning of God's word
to Hosea" *(Hosea 1:1)*. This is the beginning of the revelation of
the prophetic word to him. Here too, the first things revealed
are the Husks and their powers. These are the adulterous
woman and adulterous children mentioned in his prophecy.

Ezekiel thus ascended to heaven, and it was there that he
bound himself so as to be able to perceive, as it is written, "The
heavens were opened, and I saw visions of God." When he
reached the level of the Husks, however, he found it very
unpleasant, and did not bind himself there, but instead, rended
them apart and passed through them. Even though he did not
bind himself to these evil forces, however, it was necessary that
he see them. This is also the deeper meaning of Elijah's experi-

ence: "God was not in the noise . . . God was not in the fire" *(1 Kings 19:11, 12)*.

From there, the prophet entered the barrier of the Light of the angels. It is well established that between one Light and the next, there is a separating veil *(Pargud)*. This is the mystical significance of the *Chashmal*.

The word *Chashmal* (חַשְׁמַל) has the same numerical value *(Gematria)* as the word *Malbush* (מַלְבּוּשׁ), meaning "garment." The reason for this is because the Chashmal is a "garment" and "vessel," concealing and retaining the Lights of the angels. May God forgive me for revealing this mystery to the world. (*See* Table 1.)

TABLE 1.
THE GEMATRIA OF CHASHMAL

Chashmal			*Malbush* (Garment)		
Chet (ח)	=	8	Mem (מ)	=	40
Shin (שׁ)	=	300	Lamed (ל)	=	30
Mem (מ)	=	40	Bet (ב)	=	2
Lamed (ל)	=	30	Vav (ו)	=	6
			Shin (שׁ)	=	300
		378			378

The prophet then saw ten troops of angels, each one divided into four Chayot, as well as four camps of the Divine Presence *(Shekhinah)*. This is the meaning of the verse, "And from its midst was the form of four *Chayot*" *(Ezekiel 1:5)*.

From there he ascended further, reaching the Light [of the Quarry of Souls, and then, the Light] of the Ten Sefirot themselves. This is the meaning of the verse, "Upon the form of the Throne was a form like the vision of a Man" *(Ezekiel 1:26)*. [The "Man on the Throne" refers to the anthropomorphic array of the Sefirot.]

The Throne itself, however, refers to the Light of the Quarry of Souls. This is the mystery of the teaching, "The Patriarchs themselves are the Chariot *(Merkava)*." [34]

[The Throne is usually referred to as the "Throne of Glory,"] and it is for this reason that the soul is often referred to as "Glory." It is thus written, "That my Glory may sing praise to You, and not be silent" *(Psalms 30:13)*, and, "How long shall my Glory be put to shame" *(Ezekiel 4:3)*.

Behold, I have revealed a deep mystery to you, even including the mystery of the Chariot. This is something that earlier generations did not comprehend.

It has already been discussed that all prophets do not draw from the same root, but that there are countless such roots. In each Universe there are 600,000 such roots, this being the meaning of the teaching that "Six hundred thousand prophets rose in Israel." [35]

Moses, however, included them all, and outweighed them all. His level was so high that he was able to ascend to *Atzilut*, where he could literally see. Even Moses, however, only saw this as it was clothed in *Beriyah*, like one seeing a reflection. *Atzilut* itself is not visible, this being the mystery of the verse, "No man shall see Me and live" *(Exodus 33:20)*.

The other prophets, however, could only see *Atzilut* when it was completely clothed in the Lights of *Beriyah*. Ezekiel lived after the destruction of the Temple, and he perceived on a still lower level, only seeing *Atzilut* when it was clothed in *Beriyah*, when *Beriyah* itself was clothed in *Yetzirah*.

After this, the Lights of *Atzilut* and *Beriyah* were no longer revealed at all. This is the meaning of the teaching that after the death of Hagai, Zechariah and Malachi, prophecy came to a close, and only *Ruach HaKodesh* remained.[36]

Rabbi Chaim Vital (1543–1620),
Master Kabbalist.[37]

3

The Cherubs

In the time of the prophets, the focal point of all prayer was the Great Temple that stood in Jerusalem. The innermost chamber of the Temple was the Holy of Holies. So great was the sanctity of this chamber that no person was ever allowed to enter into it, other than the High Priest *(Cohen Gadol)* on Yom Kippur. This was part of a most impressive service, and people from all over the world would gather to see the High Priest emerge in peace after having worshiped in this inner sanctuary.

In the center of the Holy of Holies stood the Ark of the Covenant, which was made of wood covered with gold. On this ark was a cover of pure gold, and attached to this cover were two golden Cherubs. The entire structure of the Ark, its cover and the cherubs are described in detail in the Bible, and they were made under the personal supervision of Moses.[38]

But even more important was what the Ark contained. In it were the two most sacred objects mentioned in the Bible. First, it contained the two Tablets, inscribed with the Ten Commandments, which God had given to Moses. Besides this, it also contained the original scroll of the Torah which Moses himself had written as dictated by God.[39]

When King Solomon built the Temple, he constructed a deep labyrinth going under the Temple Mount, where the holy vessels could be hidden in time of danger. Foreseeing that Jerusalem would be threatened, King Josiah ordered that the Ark be concealed in this labyrinth, sealing it off so that it would not be discovered by the enemy. Thus, even to this day, the Ark is hidden somewhere under the Temple Mount in Jerusalem.[40]

The source of all prophetic inspiration was the Temple in Jerusalem, particularly the two Cherubs on the Ark of the Covenant, which stood in the Holy of Holies.[41] In describing the Ark, God told Moses, "I will commune with you, and I will speak with you from above the ark-cover, from between the two Cherubs, which are on the Ark of testimony" *(Exodus 25:22)*.[42] What was true of Moses was also true of the other prophets, and the primary influence of prophecy came through these two Cherubs in the Holy of Holies. There is some evidence that the prophetic experience, in some cases, came about through intense meditation on these two Cherubs.[43]

Each of the Cherubs had the form of a very young child with wings.[44] Even though God had in general forbidden the construction of such images, it was God Himself who had commanded that these two forms be placed over the Ark.[45] Rather than facing the people, the Cherubs faced each other, clearly indicating that they were not meant to be worshiped, but rather that they designated a place where spiritual force was concentrated.[46] The fact that the Cherubs stood on the Ark containing the Tablets and the original Torah scroll indicated that these were the source of this spiritual power.

In general, the fact that the Cherubs had the form of winged human beings indicated that man has the ability to transcend his earthly bonds. Although man is bound to the earth by his mortal body, he can fly on the wings of his soul, soaring through the highest spiritual universes. This concept was embodied in the very shape of the Cherubs, and by meditating on them, a person could indeed fly with his own spiritual wings.

In order to explore this on a deeper level, we must look at the other important places where the Cherubs are mentioned in the Bible. The first such place is after Adam and Eve were expelled from the Garden of Eden, where the Torah states, "[God] expelled the man, and He placed the Cherubs to the east

of the Garden of Eden . . . to guard the way of the Tree of Life"
(Genesis 3:24). The "Tree of Life" here refers to the most profound spiritual experience, and therefore, before one can enter
into this experience, he must first encounter the Cherubs.[47]
These Cherubs, of course, are a type of angel.

The second place where we find the Cherubs is in Ezekiel's
vision, which, according to the commentaries, is a paradigm of
the prophetic experience in general. The first thing that
Ezekiel saw were the *Chayot,* but these are later identified as
being the Cherubs. The prophet reaches the highest levels of
the mystical experience, actually transcending the bonds that
tie his mind and soul to the physical world. In accomplishing
this, he is actually approaching the "Tree of Life," and the first
thing that he encounters are its guardians, which are the
Cherubs.

The Cherubs on the Ark were meant to be a counterpart of
the Cherubs on high, and thus, in a sense, the space between
these two forms was seen as an opening into the spiritual
dimension. In concentrating his thoughts between the Cherubs
on the Ark, the prophet was also able to pass between the
angelic Cherubs, and then ascend on the path of the Tree of
Life. Conversely, when God's message was sent to the prophet,
it would also follow this same path, first passing through the
spiritual Cherubs, and then through the ones on the Ark. The
space between the Cherubs was therefore the source of all
prophetic inspiration.[48]

Through this, we can understand what would otherwise be
a rather difficult episode in the Bible involving Samuel's first
vision. Looking at the scripture, it would appear that this
vision came to Samuel without any preparation whatsoever,
almost inadvertently. There is one clue, however, that is virtually ignored by all the commentators, and this is the verse,
"The lamp of God had not yet gone out, and Samuel lay in the
Temple of God, where the Ark of God was" *(1 Samuel 3:3).*
Another difficulty here, noted by a number of commentaries, is
how Samuel could have slept in the Temple, when it was
forbidden to even sit there.

One major commentator resolves both these difficulties by
noting that the word "lie" *(Shakhav),* besides having the usual
connotation of physical lying down or sleeping, also has the
connotation of the total relaxation of the mind that comes

through meditation. What this verse then indicates is that Samuel received his first prophetic vision after intense meditation on the Ark, the place of the Cherubs.

◇ ◇ ◇

SOURCES

God told Moses that he should place on the Ark the cover containing the Cherubs making them all into one thing. In the Ark were the Tablets that God gave to him.

God said, "This will be for Me as a Throne of Glory, since it is from here that I will commune with you. I will place My Divine Presence here, and I will speak to you from above the Ark-cover, from between the two Cherubs." The reason for this is that they were on the Ark of Testimony.

This very same vision is the Chariot (Merkava) seen by Ezekiel. He thus said, "This is the Chayah that I saw beneath the God of Israel by the river Chebar, and I then knew that they were the Cherubs" (Ezekiel 10:20).

It is for this reason that God is called the One who "sits over the Cherubs" (1 Samuel 4:4, 2 Samuel 6:2).

The Cherubs had their wings outstretched, indicating that they are a Vehicle (Chariot, Merkava) for the Glory. This is indicated by the verse, "Gold for the pattern of the Chariot (Merkava), the Cherubs which spread their wings and covered the Ark of God's Covenant" (1 Chronicles 28:18). . . .

It was fitting that they have their wings spread upward, since they are a Throne for the transcendental, and they also cover the Tablets, which were written by God Himself. It is for this reason that the Cherubs were called the "Structure of the Chariot (Merkava)." This is because the Cherubs seen by Ezekiel as a vehicle for the Divine Glory were in the same form as the [physical] Cherubs, which was a form of glory and beauty.

The Cherubs in the Tabernacle and [later in] the Temple had the same form (as those on high). It is thus written, "For one above the other watches, and there are higher ones than they" (Ecclesiastes 5:7).

Rabbi Moses ben Nachman (1194–1270),
Legalist, Commentator and Mystic.[49]

◊ ◊ ◊

It is written, "Samuel lay in the Temple of God, where the Ark of God was" *(1 Samuel 3:3).* The word "in" here does not refer to place, as many commentaries think, but it refers to a concept. . . . This verse thus means that Samuel lay there, meditating *(hitboded)* on the concept of the Temple, on the place of God's Ark. When his thoughts soared through the concept of the Ark, prophecy then came to him. . . .

The word "lay" in this verse indicates that he was meditating on a certain concept, as in the verse, "Also at night, his heart does not lie" *(Ecclesiastes 2:23).*

> *Rabbi Isaac Abarbanel (1437–1508),*
> *Commentator and Philosopher.*[50]

4

Prophetic Methods

Although no explicit discussion of the prophetic method is found in the Bible, there are enough hints through which a fairly accurate picture can be drawn. Besides this, there are a number of traditions, found in the Talmud and Kabbalah that help complete the picture.

One important practice mentioned explicitly in the Bible was the use of music in order to help attain the prophetic state. A very clear example of this is found in the case of the prophet Elisha. The Bible relates that when he sought a prophetic message, he said, " 'Now bring me a musician.' And it was when the musician played, and the hand of God came upon him" *(2 Kings 3:15)*.

Another good example can be found in the account of how Samuel inducted King Saul into the prophetic society. Samuel told Saul, "You shall meet a band of prophets, coming from a high place with harp, drum, flute and lyre, and they will be prophesying themselves" *(1 Samuel 10:5)*. Through the power of the music, they were concentrating the prophetic energy into themselves in order to focus it. When they did so, they were able to make Saul prophesy as well.

Finally, we find another explicit statement regarding Asaph, Hemen and Jeduthun, "Who would prophesy with the harp, lute and cymbol" *(1 Chronicles 25:1).*

A repetitive melody is very much like a mantra, and it can be used to banish extraneous thoughts and clear the mind for the enlightened state. An important category of classical meditation is the path of the emotions, where one reaches a meditative state through the emotions, rather than through the intellect or senses. Since music can work very strongly on the emotions, it is particularly useful for this meditative method.

From some sources, it appears that the purpose of music was to prepare the prophet for the mystical state by removing all adverse emotions. In the above-mentioned case involving Elisha, a number of commentaries state that the prophet was angry at the king, and made use of the music to dispel his anger. It is from here that the Talmud derives the teaching that it is impossible to attain the prophetic state when one is in an angry mood.[51]

Some sources indicate that music was used only to initiate the prophet into the meditative state, but that when he actually attained this state, the music would be stopped.[52] Other sources state that music is the language of the spiritual world, and that through music, one actually communicates with the soul.[53]

The Hebrew word for the music used in the case of Elisha is *Nagen* (נַגֵּן). The eminent philologist, Rabbi Solomon Pappenheim, writes that the base of this word is the single letter *Gimel* (ג), which is also the base of the word *Mug* (מג), meaning to melt. The main idea of music is therefore one of melting and breaking down. As used by the prophets, the purpose of music was to melt the emotions and break down the ego.[54]

The Kabbalists note that another important role of music and song is to cut through the forces of evil, and help the prophet penetrate the *Klipot*. It is pointed out that the word *Zamar* (זמר), meaning "to sing," as well as its derivative *Mizmor* (מְזְמוֹר), meaning a song or chant, come from a root that also means "to cut." [55] Music thus cuts through the Husks of Evil, opening the way for the mind to ascend on high.

It is significant to note that another word for song, *Shir* (שִׁיר), is very closely related to the word *Shur* (שׁוּר), meaning "to see." [56] This is another indication that song and vision are related, and this is especially true of mystical vision.

A prominent Hasidic master, Rabbi Nachman of Breslov (1772–1810), notes that the mystical source of music is associated with the Cherubs, and hence, it shares the same root as the source of prophecy. These two Cherubs are said to represent the Sefirot Victory *(Netzach)* and Splendor *(Hod),* the Sefirot which are the source of all prophecy, and which are also related to song and melody. [57]

◇ ◇ ◇

SOURCES

A prophet cannot prophesy at will. He concentrates his mind, sitting in a good, joyous mood and meditating *(hitboded).* One cannot attain prophecy when he is depressed or languid, but only when he is in a joyous state.

When they were seeking prophecy, the prophets would therefore have people play music for them. We thus find, "[A band of prophets, coming from a high place, led by harp, drum, flute and lyre,] and they were prophesying themselves" *(1 Samuel 10:5).* The term "prophesying themselves" *(mit-navim)* means that they were making use of the prophetic methods in order to receive a prophetic vision.

Rabbi Moses Maimonides. [58]

◇ ◇ ◇

One must realize that a prophet does not attain this highest level all at once. He must elevate himself step by step until he actually attains full prophecy.

Prophecy therefore requires a course of apprenticeship, just as other disciplines and crafts, where one must advance step by step until the subject is mastered thoroughly. This explains what the Bible means when it speaks of the "sons of the prophets." These were the ones who apprenticed themselves to recognized prophets in order to learn the necessary techniques of prophecy.

Those who train themselves for prophecy must do so through a number of specific disciplines. The purpose of these is to bring the Highest Influence to bear on them, nullifying the effects of their physical nature which restricts it. In this manner, they attach themselves to God and bring upon themselves a revelation of His Light.

These disciplines can include various meditations, reciting certain Divine Names, and praising God with prayers containing such Names, combined in a specific manner.

The main initiation into prophecy, however, depends on the neophyte's devotion to God. To the degree that they make themselves worthy through their deeds and continually purify themselves through the above-mentioned disciplines, they bring themselves closer and closer to God. The prophetic influence begins to come on them, and they have one experience after another, until they finally attain true prophecy.

All this, however, requires the guidance of a master prophet. He must have an adequate knowledge of the prophetic methods, and be able to teach his disciples what each one must do to attain the desired result, according to each one's particular level of readiness.

When the neophyte prophets begin to experience revelations, the master prophet continues to guide them. On the basis of what is revealed to them, he instructs them and informs them what is still lacking in their quest. Until they attain full prophecy, they will require a master for all this. Even though some influence and revelation may have started to come to them, this in itself is not enough to immediately bring them to the ultimate goal. Before they can reach this, they need much guidance and training, each one according to his degree of readiness.

. . .

It is necessary to realize that the only individual who deserves the actual title of Prophet is one who has attained true prophecy. This is an individual who is certain that his prophecy is from God, as discussed elsewhere.[59] When he reaches such a level, there is neither ambiguity nor error in his prophecy.

In a more general sense, however, the title of Prophet is

also given to one who has had the beginnings of a prophetic experience and has attained some degree of revelation in a manner beyond the realm of normal human experience. Such an individual, however, may not perceive the concept unambiguously, and may therefore be misled. . . .

Those who are fully aware of the prophetic methods, however, are also completely aware of these stumbling blocks. They recognize their signs and know how one must protect himself from them until he attains true prophecy. These master prophets teach these things to their disciples, as discussed earlier. One of the important tasks of these master prophets is to bring their disciples to the truth and prevent them from being misled.

Errors such as these stem from the Corrupting Forces. These Forces are allowed to exist and function according to their ordained nature and according to the power that they were given. One of these powers is the ability to deceive people and influence people in a manner resembling genuine prophecy.

What they reveal, however, is not necessarily true. These Forces can reveal false concepts, and even produce miracles to verify them. The Torah therefore openly states with regard to a false prophet, "He will predict a sign or wonder, and that sign or wonder will actually happen" *(Deuteronomy 13:2, 3)*.

This can sometimes happen to a person against his will, and it can also be brought about intentionally.

A person, without having sought the Corrupting Forces, can experience a false vision. Even though he may have been seeking true prophecy from God, he may be exposed to this evil because of his lack of preparation and proper effort.

In many cases, however, an individual may actually desire to commune with these Corrupting Forces, striving to attain such false prophecy. He pursues these Forces, knowlingly working to attach himself to them. Through this, he hopes to gain a corrupt revelation, so that people should take him to be a prophet. He would then have the power to willfully mislead them, or to gain status in their eyes.

Included in this second category were the prophets of Baal and Astarte. They exerted themselves in such a manner and attained some supernatural knowledge, through which they were able to mislead those who believed in them. They were also able to produce miracles to verify their prophecy, as mentioned earlier.

The false prophets, however, knew that all of this came from the side of Evil, which they themselves had chosen. They did not consider themselves true prophets, but engaged in this because of the wickedness in their hearts.

Such evil, however, can also come to a person who is not seeking it. It is therefore crucial for those who strive for true prophecy to do so under the guidance of a master prophet. Only such guidance can prevent errors such as these.

This is true only before one attains full prophecy. Once a person actually attains the level of prophecy, he is able to clearly recognize true prophecy, and distinguish between the genuine and the spurious. It is impossible for a true prophet to have any doubts whatsoever.

Rabbi Moshe Chaim Luzzatto
(1707–1747),
Master Kabbalist and Philosopher.[60]

5

The Prophetic Position

For the most part, there is relatively little mention of body positions with relation to prophetic meditation and the attainment of the mystical state. The *Amidah,* the "Standing Prayer," which plays an important role in Kabbalistic meditation, is recited with the feet together, emulating the stance of the angels.[61] Other texts often speak of sitting and meditating.[62]

Another classical position found in the Bible involves kneeling with the hands outstretched. Such a position is found in the case of Solomon's prayer: "He kneeled on his knees . . . and spread his hands toward heaven" *(2 Chronicles 6:13).* Ezra likewise said, "I fell on my knees and spread my hands toward the Lord my God" *(Ezra 9:5).*

Rabbi Moses Cordevero (1522–1570), a leader of the Safad school of Kabbalah, comments that spreading the hands alludes to the fact that one is receiving a spiritual influx from on high.[63] According to the Kabbalists, this is also the reason why Moses lifted his hands when he wished to channel spiritual energy so as to defeat Amalek in battle.[64]

The position of uplifted hands also plays an important role

in the Priestly Blessing, and later literature actually calls this the "Lifting of the Hands." The *Bahir,* one of the most ancient Kabbalistic texts in existence, states that the reason for this is because the ten uplifted fingers parallel the Ten Sefirot, and can therefore draw spiritual energy from them.[65] This same position is also used by Rabbi Abraham Abulafia in one place in his meditative system.[66] Besides this, however, very little mention of this position in a practical sense is found in the Kabbalistic meditative texts.

There is, however, one position that is mentioned by several writers. This is the "prophetic position," and it involves placing the head between the knees. This position is mentioned explicitly with regard to Elijah on Mount Carmel: "Elijah went up to the top of the Carmel, and he entranced himself on the earth, and placed his face between his knees" *(1 Kings 18:42).* One of the major commentators, Rabbi Isaac Abarbanel, states that he was engaged in meditation *(hitbodedut)* while in this position.

This position was used for the intense concentration of spiritual energy. Elijah used it in order to bring rain, which had been previously withheld from King Ahab. In the Talmud, we find it used in a similar sense when Rabbi Chanina ben Dosa placed his head between his knees when praying for the son of Rabbi Yochanan ben Zakkai.[67] Rabbi Yochanan ben Zakkai was the leading sage of the first century, and ben Dosa had come to be his disciple. When Rabbi Yochanan's wife asked if Rabbi Chanina was the greater of the two, the former replied, "I am like a nobleman before the king, but he is like one of his servants." Rashi explains that a servant can come and go before a king without any appointment.

Another place where we find this position is in the case of Elazar ben Dordaya.[68] The Talmud relates that he had visited every prostitute in the civilized world, and now wanted to repent. After trying every other means, he finally placed his head between his knees and wept until he died. From the context, it is obvious that his repentance contained mystical elements, since we find him conversing with the sun, moon and mountains, asking them to intercede for him. What he finally did was pour spiritual energy into his soul to purify it of its sin, and he continued in this manner until he died.

The fact that he used this position is repenting for a sexual offense is of particular significance since the Midrash states that one reason for this position is that it places the head in conjunction with the mark of circumcision.[69] One of the reasons for the commandment of circumcision is to channel sexual energies along spiritual lines, and, as we shall see, this is one reason why it is performed on the eighth day. When one places the head in proximity to the mark of circumcision, one is better able to channel this spiritual energy to the mind, this being the point of prophecy.

It is significant to note that another allusion to this position may be found in the Paschal Lamb, which had to be roasted, "with its head on its knees" *(Exodus 12:9)*. The great Hasidic leader and mystic, Rabbi Levi Yetzchak of Berdichov (1740–1809), explains that in the order of the Sefirot, the two knees represent the Sefirot Victory *(Netzach)* and Splendor *(Hod)*, and that placing the knees in conjunction with the head releases the spiritual energy of these Sefirot to the mind.[70] It is well-established in Kabbalah that *Netzach* and *Hod* are the sources of prophecy, and therefore, this position is especially effective when one wishes to transmit prophetic energy.

We often find counterparts of prophetic methods in idolatrous practices, since in many cases, the idolators attempted to emulate the prophetic schools. A possible hint that this position was used among the idolatrous prophets is found in the Talmudic teaching that certain pagan Arabs used to "bow down to the dust of their feet." [71] The commentaries wonder at this strange practice, and find it difficult to explain the wording. However, it would appear that some pagans viewed the prophetic position, where the great mystics sat with their head between their knees, and assumed that they were contemplating their toes or the like. They adopted this practice and it gradually degenerated to the worship of the "dust of their feet."

This position was favored by at least two post-Talmudic schools. Hai Gaon (939–1038), head of the Babylonian academy at Pumbedita, describes the practices of one such school: "One must fast for a certain number of days. He must then place his head between his knees and chant many songs and hymns known from tradition. From his innermost being and its chambers, this individual will then perceive the Seven Chambers, and it will be as if he is actually seeing them with his own eyes.

In his vision, it is as if he is entering one chamber after another, gazing at what is in each one." [72]

Some five hundred years later, we find this same position used by a school led by Rabbi Joseph Tzayach, a prominent Kabbalist and mystic who served as rabbi of Jerusalem and Damascus in the mid-sixteenth century. In the introduction to his main work, he speaks of individuals who meditate *(hitboded)*, saying, "These individuals bend themselves like reeds, placing their heads between their knees until all their senses are nullified. As a result of their lack of sensation, they see the Supernal Lights, with true vision and not allegory." [73]

In general, Tzayach's meditative system is highly complex, involving magic squares and complex arrays of luminaries and chambers. His main works deal with these systems in almost microscopic detail, but, in general, the author is very reticent in describing how it can be used. In one place, however, he outlines the method, and this too involves the prophetic position. He writes, "If you wish to enter into their mystery, concentrate on all that we have said, and contemplate the chambers that we have discussed, together with their lights, colors and letter combinations. Meditate *(hitboded)* on this for some time, either briefly or at length. Begin by placing your head between your knees." [74]

He then provides a remarkable prayer that should be said while in the prophetic position:

> *Ehyeh Asher Ehyeh,* Crown me *(Keter).*
> *Yah,* give me Wisdom *(Chakhmah).*
> *Elohim Chaim,* grant me Understanding *(Binah).*
> *El,* with the right hand of his Love, make me great
>   *(Chesed).*
> Elohim, from the Terror of His judgment, protect me
>   *(Gevurah).*
> *YHVH,* with His mercy grant me Beauty *(Tiferet).*
> *YHVH Tzavaot,* watch me Forever *(Netzach).*
> *Elohim Tzavaot,* grant me beatitude from his Splendor
>   *(Hod).*
> *El Chai,* make His covenant my Foundation *(Yesod).*
> Adonoy, open my lips and my mouth will speak of Your
>   praise *(Malkhut).*

The reader will immediately notice that this chant includes the Ten Sefirot, as well as the Divine Names associated with them in the Kabbalistic tradition. This is the only place where we find an actual meditative practice involving the prophetic position. Most of these methods were restricted to small secret societies, and it is possible that this method was in the possession of the same school since the time of Hai Gaon.

◇ ◇ ◇

SOURCES

Rabbi Chanina ben Dosa once went to study Torah as a disciple of Rabbi Yochanan ben Zakkai. Rabbi Yochanan ben Zakkai's son became sick, and he said, "Chanina my son, pray for him that he may live."

Rabbi Chanina placed his head between his knees and prayed, and the son became well.

Rabbi Yochanan ben Zakkai said, "If ben Zakkai would have placed his head between his knees all day long, no heed would have been payed to him."

His wife asked, "Is Chanina then greater than you?"

He replied, "No, but he is like a servant before the king, while I am like a nobleman before the king."

Talmud, Berakhot 34b

◇ ◇ ◇

It is told that Elazar ben Dordaya did not leave a single harlot whom he did not visit. He once heard of a certain harlot on a distant island, whose price was a purse of gold coins. He took a purse of gold coins, crossing seven rivers to meet her. During the act, she belched, and in jest said, "Just as this gas cannot return to its place, so Elazar ben Dordaya will not be accepted if he tries to repent."

He went and sat between two mountains and hills.

He said, "Mountains and hills, seek mercy for me!" They replied, "Before we seek mercy for you, let us seek it for ourselves, since it is written, 'The mountains will depart, and the hills will be removed' " *(Isaiah 54:10)*.

He said, "Heaven and Earth, seek mercy for me!" They replied, "Before we seek mercy for you, let us seek it for ourselves, since it is written, 'The heavens will vanish like smoke, and the earth will wear out like a garment' " *(Isaiah 51:6).*

He said, "Sun and Moon, seek mercy for me!" They replied, "Before we seek mercy for you, let us seek it for ourselves, since it is written 'The moon will be confounded, and the sun will be ashamed' " *(Isaiah 24:23).*

He said, "Stars and constellations, seek mercy for me!" They replied, "Before we seek mercy for you, let us seek it for ourselves, since it is written, 'The host of heaven will moulder away' " *(Isaiah 34:4).*

He then said, "It depends on no one but me alone." He placed his head between his knees and moaned with weeping until his soul left him.

A heavenly voice then exclaimed, "Rabbi Elazar ben Dordaya is prepared for life in the World to Come." . . .

Rabbi said, "Not only are those who repent accepted by God, but they are even called Rabbi."

Talmud, Avodah Zarah 17a

◇ ◇ ◇

6

Divine Names

In all Kabbalistic literature, it is taken for granted that Divine
Names play an important role in attaining the mystical state.
In the Bible itself, however, there is no explicit mention of the
use of such Names, except for some enticing hints. Thus, in a
number of places, we find that an individual prophesies "in the
name *(Ba-Shem)* of God." [75] As anyone familiar with Hebrew
will readily see, this can just as easily be translated as prophesying "*with* the name of God." These phrases would then speak
of using God's name as a means of attaining the prophetic
state.

Some Kabbalists also see the use of God's name as a
method of attaining enlightenment in the case of Abraham.
The Bible says that "he called in the name of God" *(Genesis
12:8)*. This is usually interpreted to mean that he prayed in
God's name, or announced God's existence to the world, but the
Kabbalistic interpretation fits the words more literally. [76]

A very similar interpretation is given to the verse, "He
was enraptured in Me, and I will bring him forth. I will raise
him up because he knew My name" *(Psalms 91:14)*. Here, a
major commentator, Rabbi Abraham Ibn Ezra (1089–1164),

states explicitly that this means that "he knew the mystery of
My name." An ancient Midrash likewise states in the name of
the great sage of the second century, Rabbi Pinchas ben Yair,
"Why do people pray without being answered? Because they do
not know how to use the Explicit Name *(Shem
HaMeforesh)*." [77] Since this Midrash is expounding the above
verse, it is a clear indication that "knowing God's name" implies knowing how to actually make use of it.

There are other hints of the power of God's Name. The
Psalmist thus says, "Some come with chariots, some with
horses, but we utter the name of God" *(Psalms 20:8)*. The usual
interpretation is that this is speaking of prayer, but here too,
the verse can be taken literally. [78] This is particularly suggested by a verse that introduces this concept: "We will ecs-
tasize *(Ranen)* in Your salvation, and in (with) the Name of
God, we will ascend, God will fill all your requests" *(Psalms
20:6)*. As we shall see, the Hebrew word *Ranen* refers to a
method of meditation, and here we see that it also involves
God's Name. A very similar concept is found in the verse, "All
nations surround me, but with the name of God I will destroy
them with a word" *(Psalms 118:10)*.

The tradition regarding these Names of God is well established in the Talmud, and is discussed in many places. Most
prominent are the various names that the Bible uses for God,
and these are found to be ten in number, paralleling the Ten
Sefirot. [79] Besides this, the Talmud also speaks of a Name
containing twelve letters, as well as one containing forty-two,
both of which are described in Kabbalistic literature. [80] There is
also considerable discussion of a Name containing seventy-
two letters or triads, and this plays an important role, especially in Abulafia's system. [81] The Talmud is filled with traditions regarding the power of these names when they are properly used. [82]

The most important and potent of God's names is the
Tetragrammaton, YHVH (יְהֹוָה). This name is never
pronounced out loud, even in prayer. It is taught that one who
pronounces the Tetragrammaton disrespectfully is guilty of a
most serious offense, and is worthy of death. [83]

Although the Tetragrammaton is often discussed with
respect to Kabbalistic meditation, the Kabbalists likewise
warn against pronouncing it out loud. The eminent Kabbalist,

Rabbi Moshe Cordevero, writes, "If one wishes to utter the Tetragrammaton, he should do so with his mouth closed, so that no air should leave his mouth. It should not be voiced at all, but only mouthed with the larynx and tongue. Among initiates, this method is known as 'swallowing' the Divine Name." [84] Even this, however, should not be done except when one reaches the highest disciplines of meditation.

The Talmud teaches that the only place where it was ever permitted to actually pronounce the Tetragrammaton was in the Holy Temple *(Bet HaMikdash)* in Jerusalem. This is based on the verse which calls the Temple "The place that God will choose . . . to place His Name there" *(Deuteronomy 12:5)*.[85] Since the prophets apparently made use of the Tetragrammaton in attaining the mystical state, they would most often meditate in one of the chambers of the Holy Temple.[86]

The main place where the Tetragrammaton was publicly used was in the Temple, for the Priestly Blessing, as well as ten times during the public confessions of the Yom Kippur service. Whenever this Name was pronounced during a Temple service, all present would respond, "Blessed be the name of His glorious Kingdom forever and ever." [87]

On Yom Kippur, those standing near the front would also prostrate themselves to the ground, in awe and reverence of God's most holy Name. There is a Talmudic tradition that one of the miracles of the Holy Temple was that they had room to prostrate themselves, even though they stood tightly packed together during the service.[88]

Originally, the Tetragrammaton was used by all the priests in the Priestly Blessing in the Temple. The Talmud teaches, however, that after the death of Simon the Just (around 291 b.c.e.), its use was discontinued, since the Divine presence was no longer manifest in the Temple, and the other priests felt themselves unworthy.[89] As long as the Temple stood, however, it was used by the High Priest in the Yom Kippur service, but it was repeated so low that it was drowned out by the singing of the other priests. All this was so that those who were unworthy should not learn precisely how it is to be pronounced.[90]

There is some discussion in the literature as to why all these Names have such a profound effect. Rabbi Abraham Abulafia states that the Names themselves do not have any intrinsic powers, but rather, when properly used, can induce states of consciousness where the person himself has such powers.[91] The Name is therefore used primarily as a meditative device to bring the individual into certain states of consciousness, transporting him to the proper spiritual framework, whether for prophecy or to direct spiritual energy in other ways.

Most Kabbalists, however, maintain that besides this, the Names also have important intrinsic power. They are intimately attached to various spiritual Forces, and when one makes proper use of these Names, these Forces are brought into play and one can bind himself to them. Since all the Divine Names are extremely potent in this respect, one must be extremely careful not to use them except in the proper context and in the most serious manner.

One of the greatest sources of confusion is the fact that many people think that these Names need only to be recited to be effective. According to all the Kabbalistic texts that speak of this, use of the Divine Names involves much more than this. First, there is considerable preparation that the individual requires before he can make use of these Names. The Names themselves, in most cases, were used very much like a mantra. In the *Hekhalot,* a mystical text dating from the first century, we find certain Names and letter combinations which must be repeated over and over, bringing the user into the mystical state.[92] In other cases, they were repeated in combination with other letters, with an entire series of different vowel points. Abulafia's system calls for this, and also includes various body motions and breathing techniques.[93] When used as *Yechudim* (Unifications), letters of various Names had to be contemplated with deep concentration and brought together in various ways.[94]

While the Divine Names could help a person reach a meditative state when used correctly, their use had to be preceded by considerable spiritual preparation. Most important were the Ten Steps leading to *Ruach HaKodesh* discussed earlier. It is only after one has attained these Ten Steps through intense self discipline that these meditative methods can be truly effective. If one is not sufficiently prepared, he may indeed attain "enlightenment," but it will be from a source far removed from the holy.

In general, then, the proper use of the various Divine Names was seen as the key to prophecy and enlightenment. At the same time, this was also one of the most closely guarded secrets of the Kabbalah.

◇ ◇ ◇

SOURCES

Rabba bar Bar Chana said in the name of Rabbi Yochanan: The Name containing Four Letters (Tetragrammaton) was given over by the sages to their disciples once every seven years. . . .

The Rabbis taught: At first, the Name containing twelve letters was given over to everyone. When many people began to misuse it, however, it was only given over to the most modest priests. The priests would [use it in the Priestly Blessing, but would] "swallow" its pronunciation, so that it not be heard over the song of the other priests.

Rabbi Tarfon said: I once followed my maternal uncle when he went up to recite the Priestly Blessing. I inclined my ear next to the High Priest, and heard him pronounce the Name, but it was swallowed up in the song of the other priests.

Rabbi Judah said in the name of Rav: The Name containing forty-two letters is not to be given over except to an individual who is modest and humble, past the midpoint of his life, and who does not become angry or drunk, and does not insist on having his way. Whoever knows it, is careful with it, and safeguards it in purity, is loved on high and endeared below. People stand in awe of him, and he inherits both worlds, this and the next.

Talmud, Kiddushin 71a

◇ ◇ ◇

Before we go into an explanation of the details of the Divine Names, we must provide an introduction to their overall significance. Looking at many of them, one only sees incomprehensible combinations of letters, without any discernible meaning, and most of them are also unpronouncable. When an intelligent person sees such things, he can think that these names have no rational basis, and even that they involve nothing more than childish superstition, heaven forbid. We therefore have an obligation to warn the reader not to make this basic mistake.

Actually, the truth concerning these names is just the opposite. They can bring to the highest states, since they are all engraved in the loftiest spiritual realms. Their source reaches up through the steps of the Ladder, level by level, until it reaches the place where they express the essence of the Sefirot and their spiritual nature.

The souls of the letters used in these Names are the substance of the Sefirot, in their internal essence. The Name designated for each one is a garment for that Sefirah. It is for this reason that the Names [associated with the Ten Sefirot, which are the names that the Bible uses for God,] may not be erased or destroyed.

These Names and others like them were revealed to the Holy Men, servants of the Most High, as well as to the prophets, who spoke with *Ruach HaKodesh*. The tradition remained with the sages of the Talmud, in many cases dating back to Moses, who received it from God himself.

Making use of these letters, the prophets would attain a very high level of meditation *(Hitbodedut)*. They would purify their souls through the spiritual essence clothed in these letters, as well as the order of Unification *(Yichud)* that binds one level to the next. By intertwining these letters, [combining one Name with another,] they were able to perceive how the supernal Universes were attached to each other. It was in this manner that they increased their knowledge until they realized the power and purpose of these spiritual Forces. At the same time, however, they never made use of them except to understand the greatness of their Creator.

Because of the many persecutions, the eyes of the wise were shut and their hearts diminished. Those who sought to understand the Torah found themselves too weak to even comprehend simple things, and the Kabbalistic knowledge involving the details of the Sefirot was certainly above their heads. This was even more true with regard to the Practical Kabbalah, [which taught the use of the Divine Names].

No one had a treasury of power that could be used against the persecutions more than Rabbi Shimon bar Yochai [author of the *Zohar*], who, together with his disciples, revealed the hidden mysteries to the world. But because of the "shortness of spirit and great toil," his words are not understood, and our meager intellect cannot even uncover the outer edge of the depth found in his teachings. All of his words are concealed to the utmost degree. If we hammer away with our intellect, asking questions and breaking the husks that cover the doctrines, then we can see some light, through crevices as small as the eye of a needle.

The Practical Kabbalah was known in the days of such giants as Rabbi Moses Nachmanides [Ramban] (1194–1270), Rabbi Eliezer [Rokeach] of Worms (1160–1238), and Rabbi Joseph Gikatilla (1248–1305). During the period of the *Gaonim* (the seventh and eighth centuries), use was made of texts [on the Practical Kabbalah] such as the *Shimusha Rabba* and the *Shimusha Zuta*.

All this, however, was lost as a result of our sins. Those in possession of these mysteries did not wish to reveal them, seeing that those who truly loved God had passed away and that men of deeds were few, and fearing that these mysteries would be misused by those who were not worthy. We actually see that they were correct, since this happened to those who followed them in many cases. Even in recent times, there was the case of those like Joseph della Reina, who caused much misery and destruction.

For this reason, we will not delve into the use of the Divine Names, even though this can be found in some earlier texts. We will only go into those explanations that will aid our understanding.

One essential concept is the fact that all the letters depend on the Tetragrammaton. Some letters have, in essence, an allusion to this Name in their very structure. This is true of the letter Alef, which consists of two Yuds and a Vav, which when combined have a numerical value of 26, just like that of the Tetragrammaton (*See* TABLE 2). The same is true of such letters as Lamed, Tet and Kuf, which are made up of the letters Kaf and Vav.

TABLE 2.
LETTERS AND THE TETRAGRAMMATON

Numerical value of the Tetragrammaton Yud (י) =	10
Heh (ה) =	5
Vav (ו) =	6
Heh (ה) =	5
	26

Alef (א) = Vav Yud Yud (ויי)

א → אי

Vav (ו) =	6
Yud (י) =	10
Yud (י) =	10
	26

Tet (ט), Lamed (ל), Kuf (ק) = Kaf Vav (כו)

בוט → ט   כו ל → ל   כו ן → ק

Kaf (כ) =	20
Vav (ו) =	6
	26

All this alludes to the fact that the letters of the alphabet must be permuted with those of the Tetragrammaton. The vowel points must also be permuted with them, in order to bring their essence back to their Root and influence them from the highest source.

The various spiritual concepts, as well as the threads that connect them, vary according to their source. This is expressed by the vowel points.

One must therefore combine the letters of the Tetragrammaton with those of the alphabet, and both of these must be combined in every manner possible with all the vowel points. This then alludes to all the roots, since they are influenced by the highest Source.

Rabbi Moses Cordevero [96]

◇ ◇ ◇

Some of the earlier sages discussed the permutations and combinations of the Name containing seventy-two letters, as well as other Divine Names. When a pure, righteous individual makes use of these through deep meditation *(hitbodedut),* he can have revealed to him a small portion of a Divine Echo *(Bat Kol).* Regarding this, it is written, "The spirit of God spoke in me, and His Word was on my tongue" *(2 Samuel 23:2).*

The reason for this is that one can bind the spiritual Forces together and unite them through these Names ... until a powerful influx is granted to him. The only condition is that he should be worthy of this, since if he is not, the spirit can be destructive and lead him into the clutches of the Forces of evil.

Rabbi Moses Cordevero[96]

TABLE 3.

A system in which the letter Yud, the first letter of the Tetragrammaton, is combined with the letter Alef and the five primary vowels. This is used as a meditative device.

AoYo	AoYa	AoYe	AoYi	AoYu	אִי אֶי אֵי אֲי אֹי
AaYo	AaYa	AaYe	AaYi	AaYu	אִי אֱי אֶי אֲי אַי
AeYo	AeYa	AeYe	AeYi	AeYu	אִי אֶי אֵי אֲי אֵי
AiYo	AiYa	AiYe	AiYi	AiYu	אִי אֶי אֵי אֲי אִי
AuHo	AuHa	AuYe	AuYi	AuYu	
YoAo	YoAa	YoAe	YoAi	YoAu	אֹי אֵי אֶי אֲי אִי
YaAo	YaAa	YaAe	YaAi	YaAu	אַי אֲי אֶי אֱי אִי
YeAo	YeAa	YeAe	YeAi	YeAu	אֵי אֶי אֵי אֲי אִי
YiAo	YiAa	YiAe	YiAi	YiAu	אִי אֶי אֵי אֲי אִי
YuAo	YuAa	YuAe	YuAi	YuAu	

A similar system:

יוֹר　　　　　　הָא

אִי אִי אִי אִי אִי אִי　　　　אֵה אֵה אֵה אֵה אֵה אֵה
אֵי אֵי אֵי אֵי אֵי אֵי　　　　אֶה אֶה אֶה אֶה אֶה אֶה
אֶי אֶי אֶי אֶי אֶי אֶי　　　　אֱה אֱה אֱה אֱה אֱה אֱה
אֲי אֲי אֲי אֲי אֲי אֲי　　　　אַה אַה אַה אַה אַה אַה
אִי אִי אִי אִי אִי אִי　　　　אֹה אֹה אֹה אֹה אֹה אֹה
אֵי אֵי אֵי אֵי אֵי אֵי　　　　אָה אָה אָה אָה אָה אָה

וָאוּ　　　　　　הָא

אָו אָו אָו אָו אָו אָו　　　　אַה אַה אַה אַה אַה אַה
אֵו אֵו אֵו אֵו אֵו אֵו　　　　אֶה אֶה אֶה אֶה אֶה אֶה
אֶו אֶו אֶו אֶו אֶו אֶו　　　　אֱה אֱה אֱה אֱה אֱה אֱה
אֲו אֲו אֲו אֲו אֲו אֲו　　　　אֹה אֹה אֹה אֹה אֹה אֹה
אֹו אֹו אֹו אֹו אֹו אֹו　　　　אָה אָה אָה אָה אָה אָה
אָו אָו אָו אָו אָו אָו　　　　אֵה אֵה אֵה אֵה אֵה אֵה

◇ ◇ ◇

God desired to be called by a Name. Through this Name, His handiwork can speak of Him and call Him. By uttering this Name, individuals can also bring themselves close to Him.

God specified a unique Name (the Tetragrammaton) for His Glory, and regarding this Name it is written, "This is My Name forever" *(Exodus 3:15)*. To the extent that God desires to have a Name, this is His Name with respect to the Glory itself.

Besides this, however, God also makes use of other Influences *(Sefirot)*. With respect to these, He also has different Names.

God also decreed and ordained that when an individual utters His Name, divine Illumination and Influence are bestowed upon him. This is what God meant when He said, "In every place where I allow My Name to be mentioned, I will come to you and bless you" *(Exodus 20:21)*.

When a particular name of God is uttered and used to call upon Him, it results in the emanation of an Influence associated with that Name. The type of Influence transmitted will be that which God associated with the particular Name, by virtue of its mystery.

When a particular Influence is transmitted, it will necessarily give rise to the results specified for it. Its particular effects will then spread through the entire sequence of creation, from the beginning to the end.

This entire process, however, is circumscribed by the Highest Wisdom. God thus decreed that a Name should only transmit an Influence and have an effect when uttered under specific conditions in a defined manner. Otherwise, it has no effect at all.

God arranged that some of the Influences motivated by the utterances of His names should have the power of suspending the natural limitations of the one making use of them. This individual is then able to bind himself to spiritual beings, and thereby receive information and enlightenment.

This information may include things otherwise accessible to human reason. Other things that it may include, however, are the various levels of *Ruach HaKodesh* and Prophecy.

God decreed that inspiration and prophecy should be attained in this manner, through the Names associated with God

with respect to these Influences. An individual attains this
when he repeats these Names mentally, utters them verbally,
or combines them with other words, and at the same time
fulfills all the other necessary conditions.

Even though transcending the bonds of nature is a single
general concept, it obviously can occur in many ways, depend-
ing on the particular arrangement and level associated with
the method that is used. The Influences needed to complete the
process with all its aspects will also depend on the intrinsic
properties of the method, as well as its form. The number of
details and conditions involving the use of God's Names also
depend on this.

.   .   .   .

This method, involving the transmission of God's Influences
through His Names, can only be used by an individual who has
attained a high degree of closeness and attachment to God. The
greater this degree of closeness, the more successful he will be
in making use of this method. If it is lacking, it will correspond-
ingly be more difficult for him to achieve any results. . . .

It is obvious, however, that it is not appropriate for just
anyone to make use of the King's scepter. Regarding this, the
sages teach, "He who makes use of the Crown will pass
away." [97] Methods such as these are only permitted to holy
individuals, who are closely attached to God. Such individuals
furthermore only use these methods to sanctify God's name
and do His will.[98] Even though an unworthy person may not be
prevented from obtaining results if he follows the proper pro-
cedures, he can still be punished for his willful act.[99]

In any case, as already mentioned, these powers are not
absolute, but are sharply circumscribed by the limitations
defined by the Highest Wisdom. Furthermore, even within
these limits, God's decree can prevent them from having any
effect, any time that His wisdom deems this fitting and proper.

Rabbi Moshe Chaim Luzzato.[100]

7

Meditation

We have already seen that meditation was very important in the careers of the prophets. Since this fact is not very well recognized, however, it would be useful to look at a number of classical sources that speak of this explicitly. As we shall see, a good number of the most influential classical Judaic philosophers and Kabbalists clearly stated that meditation was the most important of all disciplines required to attain enlightenment and prophecy.

There are sources dating from Talmudic times which teach that prophecy involves a very high degree of mental quietude. Jeremiah's disciple, Baruch ben Neriah said, "I have not found serenity," and a very ancient Midrash comments, "Serenity is nothing other than prophecy." [101] The spiritual power and enlightenment that is the most important element of the prophetic experience is not found in the whirlwind or earthquake, but in the "still small voice" of utter tranquility. This is a state that is attained through deep meditation.

Rabbi Isaac Abarbanel (1437–1508), one of the most influential Bible commentators and philosophers speaks of meditation in the context of prophecy in a number of places. He states that the first step in prophecy is to attain a strong level of desire to bind oneself to God, and this must then be followed by intense meditation.

Elsewhere, he teaches that the prophets used to have a special place for their meditations. After Saul attempted to strike David with a spear, the scripture states that "David fled and escaped, and he came to Samuel in Ramah. . . . He and Samuel then went to Naioth, where they remained" *(1 Samuel 19:18)*. Abarbanel writes, "It appears that Naioth was a place near Ramah, where the prophets stayed. It was a place set aside for their meditations *(hitbodedut),* where they would go and seek the word of God. The Targum therefore states that it was the 'Academy of the Prophets.' "

◇ ◇ ◇

SOURCES

The prophets would meditate *(hitboded)* on the highest mysteries of the Sefirot, as well as on the Supernal Soul, which includes all attributes. They would depict these things in their mind with their imaginative faculty, visualizing them as if they were actually in front of them.

When their soul became attached to the Supernal Soul, this vision would be increased and intensified. It would then be revealed automatically through a state where thought is utterly absent. . . .

It was in this manner that the early saints would raise their thoughts, reaching the place from which their souls emanated.

This was also the method of attaining prophecy. The prophet would meditate *(hitboded),* directing his heart and attaching his mind on high. What the prophet would visualize would depend on the degree and means of his attachment. He would then gaze and know what would happen in the future.

This is the meaning of the verse, "To Him shall you cleave" *(Deuteronomy 10:20).*

Rabbi Menachem Recanti (1223–1290),
Master Kabbalist.[102]

◇ ◇ ◇

Prophecy is a spiritual influx granted by God to man. It is obvious that the individual must prepare himself for such perfection, by binding himself to God and constant meditation *(hitbodedut)* in His worship.

It is also obvious that this attachment and bond to God is attained through the Torah and its commandments, which contain the ultimate perfection of man.

The proper way of attaining this level is through true love and worship of God. It is obvious that if one strengthens this bond of love, he will be all the more ready for enlightenment. When an individual maintains this bond consistently and meditates *(hitboded)* deeply in his love of God, there is no question that the divine influx will be granted to him, providing that there is nothing to prevent it.

Rabbi Chasdai Cresces (1340–1410),
Philosopher.[103]

◇ ◇ ◇

With his keen mind, [Moses] was able to understand what was required to attain enlightenment, realizing that the path was through meditation *(hitbodedut).*

He therefore chose to separate himself from all who would disturb him and to reject all physical desires, choosing to be a shepherd in the desert, where no people are to be found. While he was there he unquestionably attained a great attachment to the conceptual, divesting himself of all bodily desires, until he was able to remain for forty days and nights without eating or drinking.

Rabbi Simon ben Tzemach Duran
(1361–1444),
Philosopher and Commentator.[104]

◇ ◇ ◇

It is written [that Samuel told Saul], "When you come to the city, you shall meet a band of prophets, coming from the high place, with harp, drum, flute and lyre, and they will be prophesying themselves *(mit-navim)*. The spirit of God shall then succeed in you and you shall prophesy yourself with them, and you shall be transformed into a different man" *(1 Samuel 10:5,6)*. . . .

These individuals were the "sons of the prophets," the disciples of Samuel. He taught and directed them, preparing them to preceive the prophetic influx. They would go to this hill to meditate *(hitboded)* and seek prophecy because of the influence of the Ark of God, which was kept there.

While seeking prophecy, they made use of musical instruments, preparing themselves through the elation produced by the music.

When the scripture says that they were "prophesying themselves" *(mit-navim)*, it does not mean that they were singing praise, as stated by a number of commentaries. Rather it means that they were inducing prophecy in themselves through meditation *(hitbodedut)*. The word *Mit-nave* is the reflexive form of the verb *Nava*, meaning "to prophesy."

The verse then says, "The spirit of God shall succeed in you." In my opinion, this means that *Ruach HaKodesh* would "succeed" in him, this referring to the will and desire for prophecy. Immediately then, "you will prophesy yourself *(mit-nave)* with them," meaning that he would engage himself in the methods of prophecy. The scripture then states that he would attain his desired goal: "You will be transformed into a different man." He would attain the prophetic influx, and through this, he would become a different person.

This indicates that the first step in prophecy is a strong desire. This is followed by meditation *(hitbodedut)*, which is its means. The goal is then the influx that comes to him.

Rabbi Isaac Abarbanel.[105]

◇ ◇ ◇

The concept of a prophetic dream and that of a vision are so close to each other that they both can be considered the same. The reason for this is that they both have the same source. . . .

Such a prophetic dream comes through meditation *(hitbodedut)* involving the mind and consciousness. As a result of the power of this meditation on a subject in the mind, a strong impression is made on the soul. Through this meditation, the soul elevates itself, just as if it were separated from the body, and it is not restrained by the physical.

This is actually the meaning of the word *Chalom* (חֲלוֹם), meaning "dream." It comes from the root *Chalam* (חלם), meaning "to strengthen," as in "You strengthened me *(tachlime-ni)* and gave me life" *(Isaiah 38:16)*. The reason for this is because a dream is caused by the strength *(chalam)* and vitality of the soul, when it overcomes the body. When one is in a state of preparation through meditation *(hitbodedut)*, he is strengthened through a prophetic dream. . . .

A prophetic vision is also the result of meditation. The prophet mentally gazes at the glorious visions involving the mystery of the Chambers on high, binding them together and unifying them on high with their Cause. His mind soars among the fearsome Forms which are in each chamber, and his consciousness is bound to them and unified with them.[106]

Through this, the prophet divests himself of the physical, abandoning all feeling and sensation associated with the body. He dissolves himself in those Forms, and his consciousness becomes clothed in them. Through these forms he experiences his vision, seeing according to the level of his perception.

It is in this manner that one receives a prophetic message, and the words are engraved *(chakak)* in his heart in a spiritual manner.[107]

After the vision leaves him, he divests himself of the Form in which he was garbed through the power of his own original form. This is alluded to in the Torah, which says, "God left when He finished speaking to Abraham, and Abraham returned to his place" *(Genesis 18:33)*. This means that Abraham returned to his original level, where he was before he had this vision.

I have seen a similar concept in the teachings of the Masters of Truth, who received it from the Gaonim. They write:

> All the faculties of the prophet and seer faint, and they are transmitted from Form to Form, until the individual is clothed in the power of the Form that is revealed to him. This power is then transmitted to an angelic Form, and when that Form is transmuted in the prophet, it gives him the power to receive the prophetic potential.
> This is then engraved in his heart with a spiritual

form that he depicts. After this agent overwhelms him, thus performing its function, the prophet then divests himself of the power of the Form revealed to him, and garbs himself in the power of his normal form. It is as if he divests himself of one form and invests himself in another.

The parts of the prophet's mind are then reunited, and his physical faculties once again return, as they were originally. Then, when he is in a normal human state, he speaks the words of his prophecy.

These are the words that I found.

Rabbi Meir Ibn Gabbai (1480–1547),
Kabbalistic Philosopher.[108]

◇ ◇ ◇

One must learn these methods from a master, just as the "sons of the prophets," who would prepare themselves for prophecy.

They would also have to put themselves in a joyous mood. This is the significance of Elisha's remark, " 'Now bring me a musician.' And it was when the musician played, [and the hand of God came upon him]" *(2 Kings 3:15).*

They would then meditate *(hitboded)* according to their knowledge of the meditative methods. Through this, they would attain wondrous levels, divesting themselves of the physical, and making the mind overcome the body completely. The mind becomes so overpowering that the physical senses are abandoned, and the prophet does not sense anything with them at all.

The prophet's consciousness is then on that which he is seeking, climbing the various orders of steps on high. It was in this manner that they would meditate and divest themselves from the physical.

Rabbi Moses Cordevero.[109]

8

The Link

From all these sources, it is obvious that meditation played a key role in the careers of the prophets, and was an indispensible element in attaining prophetic enlightenment. With the destruction of Solomon's Temple and the Babylonian Exile, however, the prophetic schools lost their influence, and prophecy virtually vanished from the scene.

A number of reasons are given for this. One is that it is well established that true prophecy can only take place in the Holy Land. While the more general enlightenment of *Ruach HaKodesh* can be attained anywhere, actual prophecy, where a distinct message can be discerned, requires special conditions.[110] Since the majority did not return to the Holy Land after the Babylonian Exile, prophecy, in its formal sense, no longer could be attained.[111]

Although the prophetic schools never admitted initiates indiscriminately, after the exile they actually became secret societies. The leaders had seen that the open quest for prophecy and the mystical experience had led many people to engage in idolatry and sorcery. In a large measure, it was this that led to the exile, and the leadership was determined that this would not recur. They therefore "nullified the lust for idolatry," restricting all mystical teachings to very limited schools, consisting only of the most spiritually advanced individuals.[112]

The entire focus of Judaism was thus altered. Where the quest for prophecy and mystical enlightenment had played a key role in the general life of the populace, it was now regulated to the background. The focus shifted, and now the Oral Law, with all its intricacies, became the focus of national life, reaching its zenith with the compilation of the Talmud. The mystical activity that existed remained the domain of a few small restricted secret societies. The general rule was, "One may not teach the secrets to two people at a time. One may not teach the mysteries of the Chariot *(Merkava)* even to one, unless he is so wise that he can understand by himself." [113]

An important ramification of this was found in the area of prayer. During the time of the prophets, there was no real formal worship service, and each person would pray in his own words. If a special prayer was needed to channel a particular level of spiritual energy, such a service could be led by one of the prophets or their disciples, who knew how to word the prayer to channel the required forces. It is for this reason that a prayer leader is called a *Chazan* (חַזָּן), from the same root as *Chazon* (חָזוֹן), meaning a prophetic vision. [114]

When prophecy ceased, however, this was no longer possible. A formal system of worship, including all of its mystical elements, had to be formulated. This was done by the Great Assembly, under the leader of Ezra, shortly after the return from the Babylonian Exile. [115] It is significant to note that a number of the last prophets took place in compiling these prayers. [116]

Many of the prophetic traditions were transmitted to the sages of the Talmud and beyond. An excellent account of this is provided by Rabbi Chaim Vital in his introduction to the *Gates of Holiness (Shaarey Kedushah)*.

◇ ◇ ◇

An Excerpt from
THE GATES OF HOLINESS

"I have seen men of elevation and they are few." [117] Certain individuals yearn to ascend, but the ladder is hidden from their eyes. They contemplate the earlier books, seeking to find the path of life, the way they must go and the deeds they must do in order to elevate their souls to their highest Root, to bind themselves to God. This alone is the eternal perfection.

This was the way of the prophets. All their days they would bind themselves to their Creator. As a result of this attachment, *Ruach HaKodesh* would descend on them, teaching them the path leading to the Light. This would then open their eyes to the mysteries of the Torah, this being the subject of King David's prayer, "Open my eyes, and let me gaze at the wonders of Your Torah" *(Psalms 119:18)*. They would be led along a straight path, prepared by the "men of elevation," so that they should reach their goal.

After the prophets came the Early Saints *(Chasidim Rishonim)*, who were also called the Pharasees (Secluded Ones).[118] They sought to follow the ways of the prophets and to imitate their methods.

These individuals would travel to rocky caves and deserts, secluded from the affairs of society. Some would seclude themselves in their homes, as isolated as those who went into the deserts.

Day and night, they would continuously praise their Creator, repeating the words of the Torah, and chanting the Psalms, which gladden the heart. They would continue in this manner until their minds were strongly bound to the Supernal Lights with powerful yearning. All their days they would do this consistently until they reached the level of *Ruach HaKodesh,* "prophesying and not stopping." [119]

Even though these individuals were on a much lower level than the prophets, we are still ignorant of their ways and methods. We do not know how these holy men served God so that we should be able to emulate them.

In the generations following these individuals, people's hearts became smaller and understanding was reduced. Masters of *Ruach HaKodesh* went to their final rest and ceased to exist among us. They left us bereft, hungering and thirsting, until hopelessness grew in the hearts of men and they ceased to seek out this wondrous discipline. All that were left were "two or three berries on the uppermost branch," [120] "one in a city, and two in a family." [121] "They seek water and there is none," [122] "for every vision has been sealed off." [123] All this is because there was no book teaching the method of how to come close and approach the innermost sanctuary.

Some bound angels with oaths, making use of Divine Names. They sought light, but found darkness. The angels with which they communicated were very low angels, overseers of the physical world, who combined good and evil. These angels themselves could not perceive the Truth and the Highest Lights. They therefore revealed mixed concepts, consisting of good and evil, truth and falsehood, as well as useless ideas involving medicine, alchemy, and the use of amulets and incantations.[124]

These too "erred with wine and were confused with strong drink." [125] What they should have done was spend their time studying the Torah and its commandments. They should have learned a lesson from the four spiritual giants who entered into the Mysteries *(Pardes),* where none escaped whole other than the pious elder, Rabbi Akiba.[126] The angels even wanted to strike him down, but God helped him, and "he entered in peace and left in peace." [127]

These individuals sought very high levels, close to actual prophecy, and it was for this reason that they were injured. But even we, today, can be worthy of the lower levels of *Ruach HaKodesh*. This can be through the revelation of Elijah, to which many were worthy, as is well known. It can also consist of revelation of the souls of saints *(Tzadikim),* which is mentioned many times in the *Zohar*. Even in our own times, I have seen holy men attaining this.

There are also cases where a person's own soul becomes highly purified and is revealed to him, leading him in all his ways. All these are ways of approaching [God], and they can be attained even today by those who are worthy. But this requires much discipline and many temptations before one arrives at the Truth. If one is not sufficiently prepared, another, unclean, spirit may enter him. . . .

I am therefore writing a book in which I will explain these mysteries . . . as I learned them from the lips of the saintly Rabbi Isaac Luria. Since these involve the deepest secrets and most hidden mysteries, for every handbreadth that I reveal, I will hide a mile. With great difficulty, I will open the gates of holiness, making an opening like the eye of a needle, and let him who is worthy pass through it to enter the innermost chamber. God is good and He will not withhold this benefit from those who walk in righteousness.

PART THREE

Verbal Archeology

1

Allusions

We have seen how meditation played an important role in the careers of the prophets, and how they experienced extremely high states of consciousness. One would therefore expect to find at least some hint of this in their writings, and in the Bible in general. If they were involved in these practices and mental states, they must have had a vocabulary with which to speak of them. Even if they do not refer to these practices explicitly, it would be expected at least that some of these words should find their way into the Bible.

Attempting to discover this vocabulary is a very difficult task. For all practical purposes, prophecy ceased with the destruction of Solomon's Temple and the Babylonian Exile, some twenty-five centuries ago. There then followed a period of several centuries during which no commentaries on the Bible were written, and very little other literature was published. Whatever vocabulary that existed to describe the practices and experiences of the prophets was, for the most part, forgotten.

Another difficulty stems from the fact that the prophets

were very reticent about discussing their practices and experiences, as were their mystical followers. There is virtually no explicit discussion in the Bible regarding how the prophets attained their enlightened state, and with very few exceptions, there is no description of their experiences. If a mystical terminology is used in the Bible at all, it is used mostly in a poetic sense, or merely in passing.

Looking for these expressions and terminology virtually becomes a practice in verbal archeology. One must dig into the Bible text, looking for promising terms, and then, both from context and linguistic analysis, attempt to discover the precise meaning of these words. In doing this, one finds the Talmudic and Midrashic interpretations, as well as the classical commentaries, to be an important aid.

The simplest way to find references to meditation in the Bible is to look at the various translations, especially the older ones, which may be based on ancient traditions. Even though we cannot rely on these translations to give us a precise rendition, they are helpful in offering clues which can be investigated more thoroughly. They might not tell us what is beneath the surface, but they can indicate where we should dig. Once we start probing, we can then fix a more precise meaning to the word.

In the classical English translations of the Bible, the word "meditate" or "meditation" occurs seventeen times.[1] Looking back at the original Hebrew, we find that in every one of these cases, one of two words is used, either *Siyach* (שׂיח) or *Hagah* (הגה). In the classical translations, no other Hebrew word is translated as referring to meditation. It would then be logical to begin our "dig" with these words.

2

Floating Distraction

The very first reference to meditation in the Bible occurs immediately after Rebecca was brought back to marry Isaac, just before their first meeting. The scripture states, "Isaac came from the way of Beer Lachai Roi . . . and Isaac went out to meditate *(suach)* in the field toward evening" *(Genesis 24:62, 63)*.

The word *Suach* (שׂוח) occurs only this one time in the Bible. It is very closely related, however, to the word *Siyach* (שׂיח), and the derivative *Sichah* (שִׂיחָה), which are also translated as referring to meditation. The Talmud recognizes this relationship, stating that *Suach* has the connotation of some type of prayer or worship, commenting on this verse, "*Sichah* is nothing other than prayer." [2]

One of the later commentaries, Rabbi Meir Lebush Malbim (1809–1879), clearly states that Isaac was engaged in a classical form of meditation. Beer Lachai Roi was the place where the angel had appeared to Hagar after she and Ishmael had been driven away by Sarah, and since an angel had appeared there, this place had become a shrine. Malbim writes, "This was a holy place at the time because an angel had been

seen there, and Isaac went there each afternoon to meditate
(hitboded)." [3] It is significant to note that Malbim uses the
term *hitboded,* which, as we have seen, refers to the "inner
isolation" of meditation.

The Talmudic teaching that *Siyach*-meditation indicates
some kind of worship or prayer is supported by a number of
verses. We thus find expressions such as, "O God, hear my voice
when I meditate *(siyach)"(Psalms 64:2),* and even more obviously, "A poor man's prayer, when he enshrouds himself, before God he pours forth his meditation *(siyach)" (Psalms
102:1).* Here it clearly refers to communion with God, and from
the first verse, it can be verbal as well. Thus, while meditation
is primarily a mental activity, the type of meditation implied
by the word *(Siyach)* can also be verbal.

In many other places in the Bible, the word *(Siyach)*
clearly refers to actual speech.[4] In later Hebrew this is certainly the case, *Sichah* being a common word for idle chatter
or speech not having anything to do with the task at hand.[5]

Still, there are also places where it refers to nonverbal
meditation, the clearest example being, "I recall my melody at
night, I meditate *(siyach)* with my heart, and my spirit *(ruach)*
seeks" *(Psalms 77:7).* From this verse we see two things. First,
it is evident that *Siyach* is a process that can involve thought
alone, where one communes with his own heart. More important, we see it related to the *Ruach*-spirit, the level of the soul
involved in enlightenment, when it is a seeking mode. The
concept of *Siyach* is thus seen as very closely related to seeking
enlightenment and exploring with one's *Ruach*-spirit.

Rabbi Abraham Ibn Ezra, one of the most important commentators, takes this as a cue. In at least two places, he interprets the word *Siyach* to indicate "conversation with one's own
heart." One place is in his commentary on the verse, "Upon
Your statutes I meditate *(siyach),*" *(Psalms 119:15),* while
another is, "On the words of Your wonders, I will meditate
(siyach)" (Psalms 145:5). According to Ibn Ezra, the connotation of *Siyach*-meditation can be to speak to oneself about God's
teachings and deeds.

There is at least one place where we clearly find the word
Siyach related to prophecy. The prophet Elisha had sent
another prophet to Jehu, a member of the king's guard, with
instructions that he overthrow King Ahab. After the prophet

left, Jehu's companions asked why he had come. The Bible then says, "Jehu came out to his master's servants, and one of them said to him, 'Is all well? Why did this madman come to you?' He replied, 'You know this man and his meditation *(siyach)*' " *(2 Kings 9:11)*. Rabbi Levi ben Gershon *(Ralbag)* explains that "it was usual to call a prophet a madman, since during his meditation *(hitbodedut),* he goes into a trance and is unaware of external events."

Although the word *Siyach* here is normally translated to mean "speech," it can equally well be translated as "meditation," as in other places. The reply, "you know this man and his meditation," would then indicate that this individual was a prophet who often engaged in meditation, and that such people were considered mad and should be ignored.

We thus see that the root *Siyach* refers to a form of meditation that can be either verbal or nonverbal. In some places, at least, the Bible associates it with *Ruach*-spirit and prophecy. Besides this, it is also a word used for casual conversation, as well as for conversation that is not to the point.

From the context, it would seem that *Siyach* refers to inner directed, unstructured meditation, whether verbal or nonverbal, around one central point. One fixes his mind on one central subject, and then allows his thoughts to caress it, looking at it from all sides. This is certainly the context of such verses as, "I will meditate *(siyach)* on Your wonders" *(Psalms 119:27),* and, "I meditate *(siyach)* on Your decrees" *(Psalms 119:48).* The general object of the meditation in these verses is God's wonders and teachings, and the mind and lips probe them from every angle.

Such meditation can also consist of singing and chanting, where the mind is allowed to wander around a particular concept. This is most probably the meaning of the verse, "I will sing to God with my life, I will chant to my God with my existence, let my meditation *(siyach)* be sweet to Him, I will rejoice in God" *(Psalms 104:33, 34).* A similar concept is expressed in the verse, "Sing to Him, chant to Him, meditate *(siyach)* in all His wonders" *(Psalms 105:1).* This type of meditation may have been associated with prophecy, since, as we have seen, music was very important in attaining the prophetic state.

Another important type of *Siyach*-meditation involves

prayer. Here the central theme of one's meditation is his own troubles or self-improvement, and again, one's thoughts are allowed to freely wander around the central subject. One's spontaneous thoughts may be verbally expressed in prayer, and this is the meaning of the above-mentioned Talmudic teaching that *Siyach* is prayer. It is significant to note that the prominent Hasidic master, Rabbi Nachman of Breslov, uses the term *Siyach* in speaking of his system of spontaneous prayer, which is actually internally-directed unstructured verbalized meditation.

An important philological analysis of this word has been made by the eminent linguist, Rabbi Solomon Pappenheim (1750–1814).[6] He states that the word *Siyach* (שׂיח) is closely related to the root *Nasach* (נסח), meaning to "remove" or to "pluck up." The word *Siyach* therefore refers to speech that is not uttered for its own sake, but in order to *remove* other thoughts from the mind, clearing it of worries, problems, and other mundane ideas. Its main connotation is therefore that of distraction, being a process intended to remove all extraneous thought from the mind.

In this context, this word is very closely related to *Hesech HaDaat* (הֶסֵּחַ הַדַּעַת), a post-Biblical term for "distraction of the mind." This term is occasionally used to indicate banishing all other thoughts from the mind so that one should be better able to concentrate on a single subject. The Talmud uses it in this manner when it says, "When we say, 'Let him distract his mind,' we mean, 'Let him distract his mind from all other thoughts but this.' " [7]

Closely related to this, and most probably from the same root, is the Biblical word *Masach* (מַסָּח). This word is found only once in the Bible, relating to the guard around the royal palace, where a third of the troops served as a special barrier: "Another third part shall be at the gate behind the guard, and they shall keep watch on the house—special duty *(masach)*" *(2 Kings 11:6)*. The commentaries explain that this "special duty" for which the term *Masach* is used, implies that they must not "distract their mind from it." [8] This means that the guards must distract their minds from all other thoughts in order to concentrate completely on the task at hand.

From all this, it becomes apparent that the word *Siyach* actually refers to a type of meditation where one removes all other thoughts from the mind, concentrating on one idea. In many cases, this can be the unstructured, internally directed meditation discussed earlier; but in a more general sense, it refers to contemplation on one idea and totally filling the mind with it. This is stated explicitly by Rabbi David Kimchi (Radak, 1160–1235), one of the most important of all Bible exegetes and etymologists. In his commentary on the verse, "Before my eyes are watches, to meditate *(siyach)* on all Your sayings" *(Psalms 119:148),* he states that *siyach* means contemplation *(hitbonenut).*

In this context, the word *Siyach* is also related to the root *Sachah* (סחה), meaning to "wipe off." This is because it is a process through which one wipes off all other thoughts from the mind.

Even more important is the fact that the word *Siyach* is also related to the root *Sachah* (שחה), meaning to "swim" or "float." The relationship between these two roots is so close, that at least in one place in the Bible, there is confusion as to which verb is intended. This is in the verse, normally translated as, "Each night I make my bed swim *(A-s'cheh* אַשְׂחֶה), with tears my couch melts away" *(Psalms 6:7).* All the major commentaries also interpret the verb as referring to swimming. However, the Targum, the ancient authorized Aramaic translation of the Bible, translates this verse, "Each night I speak of my pain." According to the Targum then, the verb is derived from *Siyach,* in its definition as speech.

In this context, both the word *Siyach* (שיח) and *Sachah* (שחה) are related to the two letter base *Sach* (סח), which means floating or rising. This is very close to the base *Saa* (שא), which expresses the concept of elevation, as in the verb *Nasaa* (נשא), meaning to "lift." As in many cases, it is also related to a base which has the precisely opposite meaning. Thus we see a close relationship between these words and the root *Shachah* (שחה), meaning "to be lowered."

So the word *Siyach* also has the connotation of floating or rising to the top of a lower level. Through *Siyach*-meditation, the individual rises spiritually, floating through the supernal Universes. Just as a swimmer floats to the top of the water, so one engaged in *Siyach*-meditation floats above the mundane world, entering the realm of the transcendental.

It is most probably in this context that the Talmud states

that Rabbi Yochanan ben Zakkai was expert in the "*Sichah* of ministering angels and the *Sichah* of demons." [9] It is highly significant to note that this is stated in the same context that declares that he was also expert in the "Workings of the Chariot" *(Maaseh Merkava)*, which, as we have seen, involves the deepest mystical states. With regard to the word *Sichah* here, the leading lexicographer, Rabbi Nathan ben Yechiel (1035–1106), states that this means that Rabbi Yochanan knew how to commune with these spiritual beings, indicating that he knew how to "float" and ascend to their realm. [10] The *Zohar* clearly states that this type of *Sichah* involves communion with the Divine Presence *(Shekhinah)*. [11]

One of the most interesting relationships involving this word is the fact that the very same term, *Siyach,* is also used to denote a bush or tree. The most obvious place where this word is found is in the verse, "Every tree *(Siyach)* of the field had not yet existed on the earth" *(Genesis 2:5)*. The eminent philologist and philosopher, Rabbi Samson Raphael Hirsch, states that in both cases, the word *Siyach* refers to growth, whether that of a plant or that of a thought. In this respect, it also has the connotation of upward motion, as does the concept of floating, discussed earlier. Hirsch explains that it also has the connotation of spiritual growth and elevation. [12]

This relationship becomes all the more significant when we realize that in many places, especially in the Kabbalistic literature, rising to the higher spiritual realms is known as climbing or ascending the "Tree of Life." [13] This is alluded to when the Bible speaks of the Cherubs who "guard the path of the Tree of Life" *(Genesis 3:24)*, as discussed earlier. It is also expressed in the verse which says with regard to Wisdom, "It is the Tree of Life to those who hold fast to it" *(Proverbs 3:18)*. The word *Siyach* can therefore logically be said to refer to ascending this Tree of Life.

It may be for this reason that God first revealed Himself to Moses in a Burning Bush *(sneh)*. The Midrash clearly relates this to the idea of trees in general. [14]

We can very often obtain an idea of the prophetic methods from idolatrous practices which tried to imitate them. When we realize how important the Tree of Life was in the context of prophetic meditation, we can also understand how the tree became a key element in a number of idolatrous practices and meditations. Particularly important in such rites was the Asherah tree, mentioned many times in the Bible. The Bible clearly denounces these rites in such verses as, "You shall not plant an Asherah, any tree, next to the altar of the Lord your God" *(Deuteronomy 16:21)*.

Realizing the importance of the tree symbolism in prophetic meditations, the idolators attempted to emulate it. They actually planted trees which would serve as the object of their meditations and visions. Through such Asherah trees, they hoped to ascend the spiritual Tree, which they most probably saw as the Tree of Life. The very word *Asherah* (אֲשֵׁרָה) therefore most probably comes from the root *Shur* (שׁוּר), meaning to "see" or "have a vision."

Hence the word *Siyach* pertains to a "tree" in its spiritual sense, where it is used as a meditative device to commune with the transcendental. This "tree" is often said to refer to the entire array of the Sefirot, and as we have seen, ascending through this array plays a key role in prophetic meditation.[15] The relationship between the concept of a "tree" and the mental process is to some extent indicated by the fact that the Hebrew word for tree, *Etz* (עֵץ), is closely related to the root *Ya'etz* (יעץ), meaning "to advise." [16]

The relationship between *Siyach* used in relation to communion with the spiritual, and its meaning as a tree, is clearly expressed in the Midrash. When Hagar and Ishmael were driven away by Sarah, the Bible states that Hagar "cast the child under one of the trees *(Siyach)*" *(Genesis 21:15)*. The Midrash states that the tree is called *Siyach* because it was there that an angel communed *(Siyach)* with Hagar.[17] It is significant to note that this took place in Beer Lachai Roi, the same place where Isaac meditated, and where the term *Suach* is first used.

The tree also symbolizes man's spiritual essence, as alluded to in the verse, "Man is a tree of the field" *(Deuteronomy 20:19)*.[18] The *Zohar* states that the "field" in this verse is the "Field of Holy Apples," a term denoting the Divine Presence *(Shekhinah)*.[19]

The word *Siyach* therefore also indicates a process whereby the individual enters into his own spiritual essence, climbing the spiritual ladder of his own soul.[20] The *Zohar's* statement that the "field" signifies a transcendental level

gives additional importance to the initial verse in which the
term *Siyach* occurs, "Isaac went out to meditate *(suach)* in the
field."

The spiritual significance of trees in this context is also
evident from the commandment to take the Four Species on the
festival of Succot (Booths). The Bible says, "On the first day,
you shall take for yourselves a fruit from the Etrog tree, fronds
of a palm, boughs of the myrtle tree, and willows of the brook"
(Leviticus 23:40). The most striking feature of this commandment is the fact that all of the Four Species are derived from
trees.

A number of sources, both Midrashic and Kabbalistic,
explain that the Four Species reflect different elements in
man, as well as different spiritual elements on high.[21] It is
particularly interesting to note that these species were taken
specifically on the festival of Succot, which was a special time
of seeking *Ruach HaKodesh.*[22] The very word *Succah* (סֻכָּה)
(plural *Succot*) comes from a root *Sakhah* (סכה), meaning "to
see," especially in a prophetic sense.[23]

The term *Siyach,* then, connotes spiritual elevation and
growth, as well as referring to the Tree, which represents the
spiritual ladder, and man's own spiritual essence. When the
individual engages in *Siyach*-meditation, he clears his mind of
all thought, and then directs it on high, floating and soaring
through the transcendental realm.

This becomes all the more evident when we closely and
literally look at a verse such as, "In Your mysteries *(pekudim)* I
will meditate *(siyach),* and I will gaze at Your paths" *(Psalms
119:15).* The word *Pekudim* (פְּקוּדִים) comes from a root
Pakad (פקד), meaning to "remember" as well as to "hold in
trust." This word indicates concepts "stored away in the heart,"
ideas that naturally exist in man's essence, but which must be
probed with insight and meditation before they can be seen.[24]
Like a "memory," they are thoughts or ideas that one holds "in
trust" for God, and in this context, the term is often used to
refer to the Commandments. In a more general sense, however,
the term *Pekudim* refers to concepts in man's own spiritual
being, through which he can reach states of enlightenment.
Thus, when one meditates on these *Pekudim,* he is able to
actually "see" God's "Paths."

Very often, especially in roots having two base letters,

these letters can be reversed and have a similar connotation. In the case of the root *Siyach* (שׂיח), the two root letters are Sin Chet (שׂח). When reversed, this yields the base *Chash* (חשׂ), from which is derived the root *Chashash* (חשׁשׁ), meaning "to sense" or "to feel." It is from this root that we derive the word *Chush* (חוּשׁ), referring to the perceptual senses. The word *Siyach* is thus very closely related to words meaning to "feel," to "sense" and to "experience," and the word itself must also be related to these concepts. Also closely related to this is the word *Chashav* (חשׁב), meaning to "think."

As mentioned earlier, idolatrous and other occult practices often shed light on the prophetic methods. According to Pappenheim, a number of such terms are derived from the base *Chash*. Such terms include *Nachash* (נחשׁ) and *Lachash* (לחשׁ), pertaining to various types of divination, in which the individual attempts to sense things that are normally hidden from the physical senses.[25] Hence the base *Chash* expresses paranormal vision, through which one gazes into the spiritual realm.

Pappenheim also notes that this same base gives rise to the word *Choshen* (חשׁן), referring to the Breastplate worn by the High Priest.[26] This Breastplate was used as a meditative device. The High Priest would gaze at the letters engraved in its twelve stones and attain a state very closely related to that of prophecy.[27] Through the *Choshen*, the High Priest was thus able to perceive beyond the normal limitations of his senses.

The base *Chash* (חשׁ) is also closely related to the roots *Chashah* (חשׁה) and *Hasah* (הסה), meaning to "be silent." The sensitivity of the mind implied by both *Siyach* and *Chash* involves a quieting of the senses and the mind, and a silencing of the normal stream of thought.

This in turn throws additional light on the mysterious term *Chashmal* (חַשְׁמַל), mentioned in Ezekiel's vision. As discussed earlier, the Talmud states that it is a combination of the two words, *Chash* (חַשׁ) indicating silence, and *Mal* (מַל) indicating speech. As such, it is the "Speaking Silence." The Kabbalists also speak of it as the interface between the mundane and the transcendental, and this is also evidenced by the context of Ezekiel's vision.[28] What it means then, is the mental state through which one passes when he ascends from the level of speaking, whether verbally or mentally, to one of pure mental silence and sensitivity. It is only after this barrier is passed that one can observe a prophetic vision, as we see in the case of Ezekiel.

The last thing that must be explored here is the difference between the two closely related words *Siyach* (שׂיח) and *Suach* (שׂוח). As mentioned previously, the term *Suach* occurs only in this one verse, "Isaac went out to meditate *(suach)* in the field." In general, the word *Suach* seems to have the same form as the roots *Shua* (שׂוע) and *Shava* (שׂוה), both meaning "smooth" and "flat." *Suach*-meditation is therefore very similar to that implied by *Siyach,* but it is a mental state that is very "smooth," ultimately calm and tranquil. While *Siyach* can be said to denote climbing the Tree of Life, *Suach* would denote resting on its highest branches.

This can be understood when we realize that this is used only with regard to Isaac, one of the Patriarchs, individuals who reached the very highest spiritual levels. Thus, while others may strive to gaze at the Chariot *(Merkava)*, the Midrash states that, "The Patriarchs themselves are the Chariot." [29] They were not like swimmers, fighting the current to ascend upstream, but like individuals smoothly floating on the still waters at the Source.

3

Directed Being

Three more words that we find indicating meditation are *Higayon* (הִגָּיוֹן), *Hagig* (הָגִיג), and *Hagut* (הָגוּת). All of these are derived from the root *Hagah* (הגה).

This root is closely related to thought, as in such verses as "His heart shall meditate *(hagah)* terror" *(Isaiah 33:18)*. Another obvious example is the verse, "May the words of my mouth, and the meditation *(hagayon)* of my heart, be acceptable to You, O God" *(Psalms 19:15)*. Rashi (1040–1105), the most important of all Bible commentators, explicitly states that Hagah means contemplation *(hitbonenut).*[30] The Midrash likewise states that "the heart meditates *(hagah).*"[31]

This poses some difficulty, since in a number of other places, the root *Hagah* clearly refers to speech. Thus we find such verses as, "The mouth of the righteous utters *(hagah)* wisdom" *(Psalms 37:30)*, and, "My tongue shall utter *(hagah)* Your righteousness" *(Psalms 35:28, 71:24)*. In this respect then, the root *Hagah* is very much like *Siyach,* having the connotation of both speech and thought. Hirsch states that the root *Hagah* refers to thought that demands expression, and therefore it sometimes exists only in the mind, while at other times it is expressed verbally.[32]

In other places, however, the word *Hagah* connotes inarticulate and repetitive animal sounds. We find such expressions as, "I will coo *(hagah)* like a dove" *(Isaiah 38:14),* and, "Like a lion and cub growl *(hagah)* over their prey" *(Isaiah 31:4).* It can denote an inarticulate sound, as in, "They make no sound *(hagah)* with their throat" *(Psalms 115:7).* It can also be a short sound or gasp, as in "Our days end as a gasp *(hegeh)*" *(Isaiah 90:9).*

On the basis of this, Rabbi David Kimchi states that the root *Hagah* indicates a sound or thought that is repeated over and over, like the cooing of a dove or the growling of a lion. The word *Hagah* occurs a number of times with respect to the Torah, as in, "This book of the Torah shall not depart from your mouth, and you shall meditate *(hagah)* on it day and night" *(Joshua 1:9).* The Psalmist likewise said with regard to the righteous man, "God's Torah is his desire, and on His Torah he meditates *(Hagah)* day and night" *(Psalms 1:2).* According to Kimchi, the meaning here is that one constantly repeats and reviews the teachings of the Torah, until they become part of his being.[33]

What is immediately suggested here is a system very much like mantra meditation, where a word or phrase is repeated many times, either verbally or mentally. This is not too far-fetched, since in the system of the *Hekhalot,* one of the most ancient mystical texts, we find that an initiate enters into the mystical realm by repeating a certain formula 112 times.[34]

In at least one place, we find a relation between God's Name and *Hagah*-meditation. The Psalmist says, "In Your Name I lift my hands . . . and meditate *(hagah)* You in the watches of the night" *(Psalms 63:5, 7).* This is also suggested by the Talmudic expression condemning one who "utters *(hagah)* the Name with its letters." [35] This could refer to repeating the Divine Name improperly as a mantra in meditation.

Another place where this is suggested is in the verse, "To speak of Your love in the morning, and Your faith by night; with a ten stringer, with a lute, with meditation *(higayon)* on the harp" *(Psalms 92:3, 4).* At first thought, it might appear difficult to see how any type of meditation can be associated with a harp. But if we think of *Higayon* as denoting the repetition of a mantra-like formula, then this can also take the form of a set of notes or a short melody, repeated over and over on a musical instrument. This itself can be used as a mantra-like device to attain the meditative state. This becomes all the more plausible when we recall that music played a key role in attaining the prophetic state.

We see further evidence for this in the fact that the Talmud speaks of the "meditation *(higayon)* on the harp," saying that the word "meditation" *(hagah)* here refers to the "reward of the righteous in the World to Come." [36] Rashi explains that in this context *Hagah* means "joy" *(Simchah)*, but, in a more precise sense, this can also denote the ecstacy of the mystical experience. This intense mystical experience is clearly related to the ultimate reward of the righteous, as the Talmud describes it, "The righteous, sitting with diadems on their heads, delighting in the radiance of the Divine Presence." [37]

Before coming to such conclusions, however, it would be useful to study the word *Hagah* etymologically as well as contextually. We immediately note that precisely the same root, *Hagah,* is used to express removal and purification. A clear example of this is, "Remove *(hagah)* the dross from silver . . . remove the wicked from before the king" *(Proverbs 25:4, 5).* Another example is, "He was removed *(hagah)* from the highway" *(2 Samuel 20:13).*

Rabbi Solomon Pappenheim, the leading etymologist, states that the root *Hagah* (הגה) comes from a two-letter base, *Hag* (הג). It is therefore closely related to another word derived from this base, *Nahag* (נהג), meaning to lead, direct or steer.[38] He then states that the term *Hagah* has the connotation of many motions directed toward one goal. These motions can be physical, but they can also involve thought, speech or sound. On a deeper level, however, it has the meaning of a meditative practice that directs the thoughts toward a particular concept.

This, together with the connotation of purification mentioned above, implies that the root *Hagah* would denote the purifying and clearing of the mind, so as to direct it toward one goal. What is particularly interesting is the fact that Plato likens this discipline of the mind to the steering of a ship.[39] The human mind is very much like a ship where the sailors have mutinied and have locked the captain and navigator in the cabin. Each sailor believes himself free to steer the ship as he pleases. First one sailor, and then another, take over the helm, while the ship travels on a random and erratic course.

These sailors cannot agree on a goal, and even if they

could, they do not know how to navigate the ship to reach it.
The task of the individual is to quell this mutiny and release
the navigator and captain. Only then is he free to choose a goal
and steer a direct course to reach it.

The Biblical word *Hagah* also appears to denote a similar
idea. One must put aside and remove all mutinous thoughts,
and allow the ship of the mind to be steered in a constant and
consistent direction, toward a well-defined goal. In this context, it is significant to note that the Hebrew word *Hegeh*
(הֶגֶה), meaning rudder or helm, has exactly the same root
letters as Hagah, meaning meditation. *Hagah*-meditation is
therefore meant to provide the mind with a rudder and helm, so
that it no longer drifts aimlessly in the sea of thought.

Another very closely related base is *Chag* (חג), referring
to anything that is cyclic or repated. It is from this base that we
derive such words as *Chug* (חוג), meaning a "circle," *Chag*
(חַג), a periodic festival, and *Mechugah* (מְחוּגָה), a compass.
It is in this sense that *Hagah* means to repeat something over
and over, periodically and cyclically, as in mantra meditation.
It is the direction of the mind that comes through such constant
repetition.

Rabbi Samson Raphael Hirsch also points out that Hagah
is closely related to the roots *Hayah* (היה), meaning "to be,"
and *Chayah* (חיה), meaning "to live." [40] Both of these words
signify a simple, elemental state of existence. Also related to
these are such words as *Hachah* (הָכָה) and *Hiney* (הִנֵּה), both
meaning "here," and denoting a basic place of existence. Like
all these words, *Hagah* is cast in the form of a single base letter
in the middle, surrounded by an initial and a final Heh (ה).

This would indicate that the term *Hagah* refers to a process that brings the mind to a state where it is devoid of all
activity. The mind thus reaches a level where it is devoid of
everything other than pure, simple, elemental existence.

What is particularly significant is the fact that the base of
the root *Hagah* (הגה) would then consist of the single letter
Gimel (ג). In his discussion of the root *Namag* (נמג), Pappenheim notes that this base suggests melting and the negat-
ing of anything solid. He states that the word *Nagan* (נגן),
meaning to "play music," also comes from this base, since
music melts the heart and immerses it in the emotions.[41] In
this context, the word *Hagah* would also refer to the negation

or "melting" of the ego. The individual then reaches a state of pure being, where he is directed by a higher force.

From all this, it appears that the word *Hagah* has the primary connotation of "Directed Existence." The individual quiets his mind to a state of pure existence, while at the same time directing it toward a single goal. The methods of *Hagah*-meditation involve the repetition of sounds, words, phrases or melodies, and it is therefore closely related to the various forms of mantra meditation.

As discussed a number of times, we can often find similarities between idolatrous and occult practices and the meditative techniques of the prophets, which the former tried to emulate. As we shall see, a prevalent occult practice called the *Oab* is closely related to the idolatrous meditative practices. So it is highly significant when we find an expression such as, "They seek the necromancers *(Oab)* and the mediums *(Yedoni)*, who chirp *(tzaftzaf)* and meditate *(hagah)*." *(Isaiah 8:19)*. It is highly probable here that the word "meditate" *(Hagah)* denotes chanting a mantra. People involved in these practices tried to emulate the *Hagah*-meditation of the prophets, and in this verse, were being mocked by the prophet Isaiah.

At this point, it would be instructive to compare the two main terms that we have discussed so far, *Siyach* and *Hagah*. Fortunately, there are two Biblical verses in which both terms appear, where they can be compared. What is particularly important is the fact that in both of these verses, the relationship between these two terms is precisely the same.

The first such verse is, "I meditate *(hagah)* on all Your works, and in Your plans I meditate *(siyach)*" *(Psalms 77:13)*. The second is, "I meditate *(hagah)* in all Your works, and in the deeds of Your hands I meditate *(Siyach)*" *(Psalms 143:5)*.

The first parallel that we see is that in both cases *Hagah*-meditation refers to "all Your works," while *Siyach*-meditation focuses on specific ideas. At first thought, the relation of *Hagah*-meditation to "all Your works" may seem difficult to understand, especially since we have defined it as a form of mantra meditation.

If we look at later practices, however, especially those of the Talmudic period discussed in the *Hekhalot*, the reason for this becomes obvious. In many cases, the forms taken by the mantra meditation discussed in this text consist of long chants, listing all of God's attributes in alphabetical order. One such chant, in its nearest English parallel, would go, "Almighty King, Blessed King, Compassionate King," and so forth through the entire alphabet.[42] Thus, at least one known form of *Hagah*-meditation actually does encompass all of God's works. It would be very interesting to explore the possibility that the *Hekhalot* may have derived this practice precisely from these verses.

Siyach-meditation, on the other hand, focused on a single set of ideas. As discussed earlier, *Siyach* refers to spiritual ascent, where one explores the transcendental realm, and one could hardly aspire to explore everything in this realm. Thus, *Siyach* cannot possibly include all of God's works. Instead, one chooses which area he wishes to explore, and then ascends to this concept. Thus, the Psalmist is actually saying, "I will ascend in meditation *(siyach)* on the deeds of Your hands."

Another significant thing that we see in both verses is that *Hagah*-meditation precedes *Siyach*-meditation. It would therefore appear that *Hagah*-meditation is a preparation for *Siyach*-meditation. This is indeed the case, since the purpose of repeating a mantra is to release the mind, so that it can then ascend and explore the transcendental realms. This is clearly seen in the methods described in the *Hekhalot,* where the initiate first chants a mantra-like device, and only then ascends through the celestial chambers.[43] When one is aware of the actual practices, these two verses take on extraordinary significance.

Another base closely related to *Hagah* (הגה) is *Gah* (גה), denoting "brighteness." Derived from this base are such words as *Gayah* (גְיָה), meaning a flame or light, and *Gahah* (גהה), meaning "to gaze."

The most important derivative of this base is the word *Nogah* (נֹגַה), referring to a "glow" or "shine." This word is particularly significant, since it usually refers to a glow shining in the dark, such as the glow of dawn or twilight. This may be a derived term, with the primary meaning being the spiritual light that one experiences during meditation, a dawn-light shining through the darkness of the mundane world. The *Zohar* thus speaks of the mystics as "transforming darkness into light." [44]

What makes the word *Nogah* singularly important is its occurrence in Ezekiel's vision: "I looked and behold, a stormy wind . . . a great cloud, and flashing fire, and a Glow *(nogah)* was around it, and from it was the appearance of the *Chashmal,* from out of the fire" *(Ezekiel 1:4).* As we have seen, the "stormy wind, great cloud, and flashing fire" refer to states of mental confusion preceding true meditative ascent. This is followed by the *Nogah* — the meditative dawn — where the prophet begins to experience the transcendental Light.

The relationship between *Hagah*-meditation and such concepts as light and fire is mentioned explicitly in the Bible. The Psalmist thus says, "My heart was hot within me, in my meditation *(hagig),* a fire burned" *(Psalms 39:4).* The visualization of light and fire as a result of *Hagah*-meditation is, then, clearly established, and this is also evident from Ezekiel's vision.

Another important thing that we see in Ezekiel's vision is the sequence. First the prophet experiences *Nogah,* the meditative Light, which results from *Hagah*-meditation setting the mind in a state of Directed Being. Only after this does he experience the *Chashmal,* the Speaking Silence, which is the gateway into the transcendental Universes. As discussed in the previous section, the *Chashmal* is related to *Siyach*-meditation. This is yet another case where *Hagah* precedes *Siyach.*

Another word closely related to the root *Hagah* is *Gahar* (נהר). The word occurs in the Bible only in relation to Elijah and his disciple Elisha.

The first place where this word is found is with regard to Elijah, where the Bible states, "Elijah went up to the top of the Carmel, and he bowed himself *(gahar)* on the earth, and he placed his face between his knees"*(1 Kings 18:42).* We have already noted that the nead between the knees was the classical prophetic position, used for certain types of meditation in Talmudic times, and up until the Sixteenth Century. The fact that the term *Gahar* is found to be related to this position suggests that it is in some way associated with the meditative practices of the prophets. According to Rabbi Levi ben Gershon (Ralbag), the term *Gahar* actually refers to the prophetic position itself.

The other place where this term occurs is in the account of Elisha's miraculous resurrection of the Shunammite's son. There the verse says, "He went up and lay upon the child, placing his mouth on his mouth, his eyes on his eyes, and his hands on his hands; and he bowed himself *(gahar)* on him" *(2 Kings 4:34)*. Here again, this can refer to intense meditative prayer, very much like Rabbi Chanina ben Dosa, who also made use of the prophetic position when praying for the sick.[45] Rather than simple worship, this was an intensive meditative prayer, designed to pour spiritual energy into the child to revive him.

This is apparently supported by the Targum, which translates *Gahar* as *Alhey* (אֱלְהֵי).[46] This comes from the root *Lahah* (להה), a biblical word found in such verses as, "Egypt was confounded *(Lahah)*" *(Genesis 47:13)*. According to the main commentaries, the word *Lahah* has the connotation of negation of the senses, the draining of strength, and the transition of being into non-being.[47] Hence, it is related to the word *Lo* (לא), meaning "no," which indicates total negation.

According to the Targum, then, the meaning of the word *Gahar* would be to indicate the negation of the self and the loss of conscious perception, as occurs in high meditative states. It was through the spiritual power that one can transmit while in such a state that Elijah was able to bring rain while on Mount Carmel, and Elisha was able to ressurect the child. This method is discussed to some extent by the Hasidic masters.[48]

4

Explosive Emotions

Another important word that expresses a type of meditative practice or state is the root *Ranan* (רנן), and its derivative *Rinah* (רִנָּה). Initially, one would not even think of exploring this word, since it is usually translated as "rejoicing," "singing," or "crying out." There is, however, one important clue, and this is the fact that the Targum consistently translates *Hagah* as *Ranan*. So, at least in Aramaic, *Ranan* has the connotation of meditation. Since Hebrew and Aramaic are very closely related languages, this at least suggests that this root be explored in Hebrew.

An excellent analysis of this word is provided by both Pappenheim and Hirsch.[49] They both indicate that it refers to strong feelings of emotion, exultation and ecstasy, which may then break out into verbal expression. It is obvious, in some cases at least, that *Rinah* denotes verbal expression, as in the verse, "The tongue of the dumb shall sing forth *(ranan)*" *(Isaiah 24:14)*.

Such expression, however, is usually accompanied by an outbreak or explosion of emotions. It is for this reason that the word *Patzach* (פצח), is only found in connection with the verb

Rinah, as in, "Break out *(patzach)* in ecstasy *(rinah)*" *(Isaiah 54:1).*[50] The verb *Patzach,* usually translated as "breaking out" emotionally, is closely related to the roots *Patzah* (פצה), meaning "to open," and *Patzatz,* (פצץ), "to explode." The term *Rinah,* therefore, speaks of emotions that can explode into verbal expression or song.

The emotions can be those of sadness, as in, "Rise, cry out *(ranan)* in the night" *(Lamentations 2:19),* which speaks of mourning for the destruction of Jerusalem. The term can also indicate the solemn feelings, often shadowed by distress and danger, expressed in a prayer, as in such verses as, "O God, pay heed to my cry *(rinah)*" *(Psalms 17:1).* At other times, it can mean the expression of powerful emotions of joy, as in, "Sing forth *(ranan),* O daughter of Zion . . . be glad and rejoice with all your heart" *(Zephaniah 3:14).*

The root *Ranan* is occasionally related to a vision of God, as in the verse, "There came forth a fire from before God . . . and when all the people saw it, they became ecstatic *(ranan)* and they fell on their faces" *(Leviticus 9:24).* An even clearer example is the verse, "Let the righteous be ecstatic in God" *(Psalms 33:1).* The Midrash comments that this verse "does not say that the righteous should be ecstatic *(ranan) to* God, but *in* God. It therefore refers to an ecstasy resulting from seeing a vision of God." [51]

From all this, it appears that the word *Ranan* refers to the way of the emotions, a meditative technique where one binds himself to the Divine with all of his emotions. One attains the mystical state by contemplating God's greatness, building up ecstasy and explosive emotions, until the soul breaks free to commune with God. It is a path described by Maimonides, when he says that the individual's heart overflows with love as a result of his contemplation on God.[52] This connotation is most lucidly expressed in the verse, "My soul yearns, it pines for the courts of God; my heart and flesh become ecstatic *(ranan)* to the Living God" *(Psalms 84:3).*

This interpretation of the word *Rinah* is expressed most clearly by the leading Hasidic master, Rabbi Schneur Zalman of Liadi (1745–1813), founder of the Habad school. He writes, *"Rinah* is the revelation of the Soul's great yearning, where it longs and pines to attach itself to God, and to include itself in the Infinite Light *(Or Ain Sof)."* [53]

We also see that the verb *Ranan* refers to a state of

clarified and awakened consciousness. The Psalmist states, "God awoke like one who slept, like a warrior clearing his senses *(mit-ranan)* from wine" *(Psalms 78:65)*. The emotional path implied by the word *Ranan* thus has as its goal an awakening and expansion of the consciousness. In his normal state, man is like one whose senses have been dulled by strong drink. Through the process of *Ranan*-meditation, his senses are cleared, and in a spiritual sense, he is awakened.

There is one highly significant parallel between *Ranan*-meditation and *Siyach*-meditation. In one verse, we find the expression, "For You, O God, have gladdened me through Your works, I will be ecstatic *(ranan)* in the work of Your hands" *(Psalms 92:5)*. Another verse discussed earlier, involving *Siyach*-meditation, states, "I meditate *(siyach)* in the work of Your hands" *(Psalms 143:5)*. It has been shown that *Siyach*-meditation involves the actual exploration of the spiritual Universes, which are the "work of God's hands," and so it would appear that this is also true of *Ranan*-meditation. The path of the emotions is also one through which one can ascend on high and perceive the Divine.

There is one place where we see a clear relationship between *Hagah*-meditation and *Ranan*-meditation. The Psalmist declares *(Psalms 63:5–9)*:

> I will bless You with my life,
> With Your Name, I lift my hands;
>> My soul is sated with marrow and fat,
>> With ecstatic *(ranan)* lips,
>> My mouth sings praise.
> I recall You on my couch,
> Meditate *(hagah)* You in the night watches;
>> For You have been my help,
>> In the shadow of Your wings,
>> I am ecstatic *(ranan)*.
> My soul binds itself following You,
> Your right hand supports me.

Here we see that *Ranan*-meditation can both precede and follow *Hagah*-meditation. One begins by arousing the emotions with songs of praise, which is the initial process of *Ranan*-meditation. When he is in such an emotionally aroused state, he can then engage in *Hagah*-meditation, which has been described earlier.

After this, one can once again involve himself in *Ranan-*

meditation, but on a much higher level. At this state, he elevates himself through the emotions, ascending on high into the spiritual realm. It is in this second context of *Ranan* that the Psalmist says, "In the shadow of Your wings, I am ecstatic *(ranan)*." Through *Ranan*-meditation, the path of the emotions, he rises to the spiritual heights characterized as "the shadow of God's wings."

The final result of this is attachment to God, described by the Psalmist when he says, "My soul binds itself *(davek)* following You." In the entire book of Psalms, this is the only reference to *Devekut*, the spiritual binding of oneself to God. Such *Devekut* (attachment) is an important aspect of enlightenment, where one binds himself to the Divine, and it is discussed at length in the Kabbalistic and Hasidic texts. It involves the creation of a strong spiritual bond between man and God, and it is through this bond that one becomes worthy of enlightenment.

There is another, similar case in which we find the ecstatic path of the motions expressed by *Ranan* as in introduction to *Hagah*-meditation. This is where the Psalmist sings *(Psalms 71:22–24)*:

> I will thank You with the lute,
>> For Your truth, O my God.
> I will play to You on the harp,
>> O Holy One of Israel.
> Ecstatic *(ranan)* are my lips,
>> For I sing hymns to You
>> As does my soul
>> That You redeemed.
> Also all day long
>> My tongue chants *(hagah)* Your righteousness,
> For they are abashed, they are ashamed.
>> Those who wished me evil.

Here again we see that *Ranan*-meditation precedes *Hagah*-meditation. The path of the emotions is closely related to music, involving the lute and the harp, just as with the prophets. We see that *Ranan*-meditation begins in the lips, but then extends to the ecstasy of the soul.

Besides all this, one of the most important things that may be learned from this Psalm is the fact that *Ranan*-meditation is a potent means of releasing spiritual forces against one's enemies. The very emotions that one evokes toward the spiritual can also serve as a means of protection against those who harbor evil emotions toward him.

A clear example of this is found in the verse, "We are ecstatic *(ranan)* in Your salvation, with the name of God, we raise our banner" *(Psalms 20:6).* This clearly refers to the use of *Ranan*-meditation as a protective device, possibly also involving God's name, as the Psalm concludes, "Some come with horses, some with chariots, but we utter the name of the Lord our God. They are bowed and humbled, but we rise and stand upright" *(Psalms 20:8, 9).*

A similar concept is also expressed in the Psalm, "Let saints rejoice in Glory, they are ecstatic *(ranan)* on their beds. Uplifting praise of God is in their throats, a two-edged sword in their hands" *(Psalms 149:5, 6).* Here again, the ecstasy of *Ranan*-meditation serves as both protection and as a weapon.[54]

Even though *Ranan*-meditation or *Rinah* is directed at creating an emotional bond with God, it also has the effect of making one's prayers for his own needs more effective. This is especially true when *Rinah* precedes such prayer, as Solomon said, "To listen to the ecstasy *(rinah)* and to the prayer" *(1 Kings 8:28).* The Midrash states that "*Rinah* is the praise of God, while prayer *(tifillah)* relates to the needs of man." [55] From this same verse, the Midrash also derives the rule that *Rinah* must precede formal prayer. Even today, this is expressed in the daily prayer service, where the recitation of the Biblical Praises *(Pesukey DeZimra)* precedes the formal prayer, which is the Amidah. From the context of the verse, it is obvious that *Rinah* makes prayer more likely to be heard by God. One reason for this is that it tears through the spiritual barriers separating man from the spiritual, as discussed by the Kabbalists.[56]

5

Blind Rapture

Another term which the Bible uses for a type of meditation is also not immediately apparent. This is the word *Shasha* (שעשע). There would be no hint at all that this refers to meditation were it not for the fact that it is often found in proximity to other words denoting meditation, particularly *Siyach*. Usually translated as "delight" or "play," *Shasha* can be identified as a form of meditation both on contextual and etymological grounds.

According to most authorities, the word *Shasha*, an unusual four-letter root, is actually derived from the root *Sha'a* (שעע) or *Shua* (שוע), meaning "to be blind." [57] This root is found in such verses as, "Make their ears heavy and blind *(sha'a)* their eyes" *(Isaiah 6:10)*. One connotation of the word *Shasha* is to be blind and oblivious to all outer concerns, as in the verse, "Trouble and anguish have found me, but Your commandments are my rapture *(shasha)*" *(Psalms 119:143)*.

Another word to which this is very closely related, however, is *Sha'ah* (שעה), meaning "to pay attention," or "to direct the attention," as in the verse, "To Cain and his offering [God] did not pay attention *(sha'ah)*" *(Genesis 4:5)*. Closely related to this is also the root *Yesha* (יְשַׁע), meaning "to seek help," since the person in trouble directs all of his attention toward his would-be rescuer. It is from this latter root that the word *Yeshua* (יְשׁוּעָה), "salvation," is derived. It is significant to note that both words occur in a single verse, "I long for Your salvation *(yeshua)*, O God, Your Torah is my rapture *(shasha)*" *(Psalms 119:174)*.

The word *Shasha* therefore denotes rapt attention, where one is oblivious to all outside influence. The one verse that leads many commentators to translate *Shasha* to mean "play" or "delight" is, "A child shall play *(shasha)* by a cobra's den" *(Isaiah 11:8)*. The actual meaning of this verse, however, is "A child shall be enraptured by a cobra's den." This means that the child will sit there in rapt attention, oblivious to all danger, and he still will not be harmed in any way. It is used here in a borrowed sense, taken from its original meditative context.

Another root to which this is very closely related is *Shua* (שׁוּעַ), meaning "smooth." As discussed by Rabbi David Kimchi, the word *Sha'ava* (שַׁעֲוָה) for wax is derived from this root.[58] This word is also related to *Shaveh* (שָׁוֶה), meaning "smooth" and "even." As discussed earlier in relation to *Suach* (שׂוּח), this term, when used to describe a mental state, describes a very high degree of serenity and calmness. Hirsch also says this in his commentary on the verse, "When my thoughts were at war within me, Your comforts soothed *(shasha)* my soul" *(Psalms 94:19)*.

One of the goals of *Shasha*-meditation is to attain a sense of tranquility, oblivious to all outside influences. As such, it is the exact opposite of *Ranan*-meditation, where one brings all of his emotions into battle. *Shasha*-meditation, on the other hand, is used to utterly divorce oneself from outside troubles, setting up a barrier of spiritual protection. This is obvious from a number of previously quoted verses, as well as from "If not that Your Torah was my rapture *(shasha)*, I would have perished in my affliction" *(Psalms 119:92)*.

One thing that we immediately see is that the object of *Shasha*-meditation is almost always expressed in terms of God's Torah or commandments. While other types of meditation can also focus on other concepts, *Shasha* consistently relates to God's revealed word. This can be readily understood in terms of the doctrine, widely expressed in Kabbalah sources, that the Torah and its commandments involve the highest of all mysteries, emanating from the very Will and Wisdom of God.[59] The term *Shasha* then denotes serene enraptured meditation on these most lofty concepts.

Another thing that we find is that *Shasha* is closely associated with the love of God. The clearest expression of this is the verse, "Your love shall come to me and I will be vitalized, for Your Torah is my rapture *(shasha)*" *(Psalms 119:77)*. Another example is, "I enrapture myself *(shasha)* in Your commandments, which I love" *(Psalms 119:47)*. The term *Shasha* is therefore closely related to the absolute love of God and His teachings, and it is seen as a product of this intense passion.

The simple form of this word, *Shah* (שׁעה), is often used with respect to a vision of God. In a negative sense, we find this in the verse, "They do not turn *(shah)* to the Holy One of Israel, they do not seek God" *(Isaiah 31:1)*. From this it immediately appears that the word *Shah* involves a type of mystical seeking of God. This is further evidenced from the verse, "On that day, a man shall turn *(shah)* to his Maker, his eyes shall see the Holy One of Israel" *(Isaiah 17:7)*. From verses such as these, it is evident that *Shah,* and its derivative *Shasha* involve a direct vision of the Divine.

There are two places where we find *Shasha* and *Siyach* in conjunction. The first is, "In Your mysteries *(pekudim)* I meditate *(siyach)*, and I will gaze at Your paths. In Your decrees I enrapture myself *(shasha)*, I will not forget Your word. . . . Uncover my eyes that I may behold the wonders of Your Torah" *(Psalms 119:15–18)*. In this verse we also clearly see that the object of *Shasha*-meditation is to bring one to gaze into the mysteries implied by the Torah and its commandments.

The second parallel is the verse, "Your servant meditates *(siyach)* on Your decrees; also Your testimonies are my rapture *(shasha)*, the men of my counsel" *(Psalms 119:23, 24)*. Here again we see the two words in conjunction, and again, *Siyach* precedes *Shasha*. We also note that in *Shasha*-meditation, the "testimonies," which refer to commandments with a special lesson, become personified and become "the men of my counsel." When an individual is on this level, he does not see the commandments as abstract laws, but as personal forces, which can teach and counsel.

An important thing that we see in both of these passages is

that *Shasha*-meditation follows *Siyach,* and it therefore very likely involves a more advanced state, leading to higher levels. When one is on the level of *Siyach,* he is floating and ascending. The level of *Shasha,* on the hand, relates to having attained the goal, and being utterly enraptured by it. It is the utter serenity that one experiences when he reaches the highest spiritual levels and is able to meditate on the level itself.

In a number of places the grammarians point out that the doubled form, of which *Shasha* (שַׁעֲשַׁע) is an example, indicates the idea of something that is rapidly repeated. Other example are *Tzaftzef* (צַפְצֵף), "to chirp," *Tzaltzel* (צַלְצֵל), "to tinkle," and *Afef* (עַפְעֵף), "to flutter," the last word coming from the root *Auf* (עוּף), meaning "to fly." [60]

The word *Shasha* would then denote a constant oscillation of concentration, a continuous turning on and off of one's attention.

Shasha represents the highest levels of meditation, and it is significant to note that the Kabbalists speak of a similar concept on the highest levels of meditation. In his vision, Ezekiel says, "The Chayot ran and returned, like a vision of a lightning flash" *(Ezekiel 1:14).* The Kabbalists point out that this does not refer to the Chayot themselves, but to Ezekiel's vision. He was on such a high level that he could not sit with a constant gaze. He had to "run and return." He would gaze at the Chayot, seeing them like a "lightning flash," and then he would immediately return, lest he become swallowed up in his vision.

This is best expressed in the *Sefer Yetzirah (Book of Creation),* one of the most ancient and mysterious Kabbalah texts. It states:[61]

> Ten Sefirot of Nothingness,
> Their gazing is like "a vision of a lightning flash,"
> Their end has no limit,
> And they speak of them "running and returning."

The commentaries explain that when one gazes at the Sefirot, he can only do so for an instant, seeing them like a "lightning flash." One who reaches this level may not remain there for more than an instant. He must run forward and immediately return, casting the barest glimpse at the highest infinite levels. A later mystic, the Hasidic master, Rabbi

Nachman of Breslov (1772–1810), speaks of this with regard to the Infinite Being *(Ain Sof)*. He says that this is a Light that is so high that one can only reach it by "touching and not touching," fluttering back and forth, so as not to perish within it.[62]

This also appears to be the meaning of *Shasha*. It is a rapt attention, where one is oblivious to all outside influences, gazing at the highest spiritual levels. But it also involves a concept of "running and returning," gazing and then averting the gaze, for a mortal human being cannot constantly keep his concentration on these levels without perishing.

6

Contemplation

The last word which we will explore in some depth is also one of the most obvious. The word *Hitbonenut,* meaning "contemplation," is used in later literature to denote this idea, and in the Bible it is used in the same sense.

This word, *Hitbonenut* (הִתְבּוֹנְנוּת), is the reflexive of the root *Bin* (בִּין), meaning "to understand." It is from this root also that the word *Binah* (בִּינָה), meaning "understanding," is derived. *Hitbonenut* literally means "making oneself understand," that is, contemplating something so deeply and completely that one makes himself understand it in all its aspects.

The connotation of *Hitbonenut*-contemplation is to gaze and stare at something, either visually or mentally, until one understands it thoroughly. We see it in the sense of visualization in such verses as, "I have made a covenant with my eyes, should I then comtemplate *(hitbonen)* a maiden" *(Job 31:1)*. It also refers to thinking over a statement, as when Job said, "I have contemplated you" *(Job 32:12)*, indicating that he had contemplated what they had said.

This word is also used with respect to God, and in this sense, it is often a preparation for the mystical state. We thus find such verses as, "Contemplate *(hitbonen)* the wonders of God" *(Job 37:14),* and, "Contemplate the love of God" *(Psalms 107:43).*

Most important from our point of view, are the verses *(Psalms 119:95, 96):*

> The wicked waited to destroy me,
> I contemplated Your testimonies;
> I have seen a purpose to every end,
> Your commandment is very broad.

Here the psalmist is saying that from contemplating on the testimony-commandments, he is able to perceive their breadth and true significance.

In general, the word *Binah* (בִּינָה) is very closely related to the word *Beyn* (בֵּין), meaning "between." Understanding *(Binah)* is then the act of separating something in one's mind, examining it by itself. The reflexive, *Hitbonen,* thus means to cause oneself to separate something in his mind. He looks at it as separated from all other things in the world, making it fill his mind completely.

Binah is also related to the root *Banah* (בנה), meaning to "build," this also being the root of *Even* (אֶבֶן), a stone, and *Levanah* (לְבֵנָה), a brick. Through Understanding, one is able to build on a concept, making use of his deductive reason to derive one concept from another, until he creates an entire structure. The Talmud therefore says that, "Understanding relates to understanding one thing from another." [63] The word *Hitbonen* is used in the sense of contemplation, since when one does this, he builds upon the object of his contemplation, using it as a springboard to higher states of consciousness

◇ ◇ ◇

SOURCES

What is the way to love and fear God? When a person contemplates *(hitbonen)* His great, wondrous deeds and creations, seeing through them His boundless, infinite wisdom, he immediately loves, exults, and is ecstatic with a passion to know the great Name. This is what King David meant when he said, "My soul thirsts for God, for the living Deity" *(Psalms 42:3)*.

When one thinks about these things, he immediately becomes awed and abashed. He realizes that he is but an infinitisimal creature, lowly and unenlightened, standing with his diminutive, deficient mind before the Perfect Mind. David thus said, "When I see Your heavens, the work of Your fingers . . . what is man that You consider him?" *(Psalms 8:4, 5)*.

Moses Maimonides.[64]

◇ ◇ ◇

What is a fitting love? This means that one must love God with a tremendous, powerful passion, so that his soul is bound to this love of God. He is constantly absorbed by it, like one who is lovesick, whose mind cannot be distracted from his beloved. He is constantly immersed in such love, whether he is sitting or standing, eating or drinking.

Those who truly love God must be continually immersed in this passion even more than this. God thus commanded us, "[You shall love the Lord your God] with all your heart, with all your soul, [and with all your might]" *(Deuteronomy 6:5)*. [In his great love song to God, King Solomon likewise said, "I am lovesick" *(Song of Songs 2:5)*. The entire book of the Song of Songs is an allegory to this love.

Moses Maimonides.[65]

◇ ◇ ◇

Contemplation *(Hitbonenut)* involves intense concentration on the depth of a subject, where one grasps it very strongly until he understands it completely, with all its parts and details. This is the innermost sense of Understanding *(Binah)*. . . .

A person can look at something, but not concentrate on it at all. He does not look at its quality, nature, and details, whether internal or external, except in a cursory manner. Because of this he will certainly forget it in time, and [even immediately,] he is only able to describe it in the most general terms. The reason for this is that he only saw it with a passing glance, and not in a manner that would leave a strong impression.

The same is true of the eye of the intellect. It can pass over a subject or idea, merely glancing at it, but not stopping or hesitating to delve into it completely. The depth of this concept is then not grasped at all. . . .

The depth of a subject, as well as its implications regarding higher concepts, are both derived from the depths of its intrinsic point. The intrinsic point from which it springs is called Wisdom.

It is written, "A river emerged from Eden" *(Genesis 2:20)*. Understanding *(Binah)* is called a river, while Wisdom *(Chakhmah)* is a fountain, as the Masters have taught.

[The Hebrew word for "fountain," *Eyin* (עַיִן), is also the word for "eye."] This [Eye] lingers on a subject and concentrates on it deeply, hesitating and not hurrying on. This is necessary if one is to reach the inner intrinsic depth of a concept, in its innermost sense.

This is like gazing at something with one's eye. One does not merely glance at the object, but makes use of his powers of perception so that it will make a lasting impression. He spends much time looking at it, until he knows it well, in its smallest details and most intrinsic essence. This is what is called contemplation *(hitbonenut)*.

Contemplation thus includes two elements. One is contemplating a thing, concentrating on it at length. Rashi explains that contemplation means to grasp the essence of a subject and understand it fully.[66]

Such concentration only pertains to the depth of Understanding derived from Understanding itself. . . .

Higher than this is the concept of "Probing," through which one can reach even higher than Wisdom.

Wisdom is the concept of Nothingness in an idea. This is the state in which it exists before it comes to the level . . . where it can be grasped by Understanding. In this respect, it is very much like the fountain or spring which is the source of a river.

Beyond this, there is an idea of Probing the depth of an idea. The root of this reaches down to the source from which the fountain or spring emanates. This Source is called the "Depth of Wisdom," or the "Hidden Nature of Wisdom." [67]

> *Rabbi Dov Baer of Lubavitch,*
> *The "Middle Rabbi" (1774–1827),*
> *Hasidic Master.*[68]

◇ ◇ ◇

7

The Psalms

Looking at these terms relating to meditation and contemplation, it immediately becomes obvious that many are found in the Psalms, often in a sense where they most strongly suggest higher states of consciousness. This is particularly true of the 119th Psalm, from which we have already quoted a number of passages highly suggestive of meditative states. This would suggest that in Biblical times the Psalms played an important role in the meditative disciplines.

It would therefore be of some interest to make an etymological analysis of the Hebrew name for the Psalms, which is *Tehillim* (תְּהִלִּים). This comes from the root *Halal* (הלל), which is normally translated as "to praise." The Psalms are therefore most often simply viewed as nothing more than a series of praises to God.

The root *Halal*, however, has two other meanings which are very significant from our viewpoint. The first is that of brightness and shining, as in the verses, "Behold the moon does not shine *(halal)*" *(Job 25:5)*, and, "When [God's] lamp shined *(halal)* over my head" *(Job 29:3)*. The second connotation is that of madness, as in the noun *Holelut* (הוֹלֵלוּת),

referring to the demented state in many places in the Bible.[69]

This would therefore indicate that the word *Halal* denotes a state where one leaves his normal state of consciousness, and at the same time, perceives spiritual Light. It is distinguished from the many other Hebrew terms for praise, since *Halal* is praise designated for attaining enlightenment through a state of oblivion.

The relationship between enlightenment and madness should not be too difficult to understand, since the Bible explicitly relates madness to prophecy. In one place, a prophet is called a madman, and the leading commentator, Rabbi Isaac Abarbanel, comments, "They called him mad, since as a result of his meditation *(hitbodedut),* he appeared demented, not paying attention to mundane affairs." [70]

In another place we find an even more explicit parallelism. God says, "Every man who is mad, who prophesies, shall be put in the stocks" *(Jeremiah 29:26).* Here again, the commentaries, most notably Rabbi David Kimchi, state that many people considered the prophets to be mad because of their unusual actions. It was not unusual then, to use the term "prophet" as a synonym for madman.

The word *Halal* is thus related to the roots *Lahah* (להה) and *Lo* (לא), which, as discussed above, denote states of negation. It is also related to the root *Chalal* (חלל), meaning hollow, especially in a spiritual sense. Such a level of "hollowness" is closely related to prophecy, this being the level of King David, who said of himself, "My heart is hollow *(chalal)* within me" *(Psalms 109:22).*

All this indicates that *Halal* denotes negation of the senses and ego in the quest of enlightenment. The Psalms were therefore called *Tehillim* because they were especially designed to help one attain this exalted state.

This philological analysis might not be conclusive if it were not backed up by a solid tradition. In the Talmudic tradition there is a clear indication that the Psalms were used to attain the state of enlightenment called *Ruach HaKodesh.*

If one looks at many Psalms, one sees that they begin with either the phrase, "A Psalm of David" *(Mizmor LeDavid)* or "Of David, a Psalm" *(LeDavid Mizmor).* The Talmud states that when a Psalm begins with the phrase, "Of David, a Psalm," this indicates that he recited the Psalm after he had attained *Ruach HaKodesh.* But when the Psalm begins with "A Psalm of David," it means that David actually made use of the Psalm in order to attain his state of enlightenment.[71] Thus at least eighteen of the Psalms were specifically composed as a means of attaining higher states of consciousness.

There is another intriguing statement regarding Psalms 90 to 100 in a Midrash. Psalm 90 is "A prayer of Moses," and according to tradition, all eleven Psalms from 90 to 100 were also written by Moses. The Midrash notes that, "Moses said these eleven Psalms in the technique of prophecy." [72] Although the interpretation is not conclusive, the Midrash may be teaching that these eleven Psalms were meant to be used as a means of attaining prophecy.

The Midrash goes on to say, "Why were these Psalms not written in the Torah [since they were written by Moses]? Because one deals with Law, and the other with Prophecy." The Torah must deal primarily with Law, while things dealing with prophecy and mysticism have their proper place in the Book of Psalms.

Upon close examination, we find that there is some additional evidence to support this. The Talmud states that Psalm 91, one of these eleven, is called the "Psalm of the Stricken Ones." [73] The Midrash states that when Moses ascended into the spiritual realm on Mount Sinai, he recited this Psalm in order to be protected from the forces of Evil.[74] Hai Gaon (939–1038), one of the important early masters of the mystical arts, writes that these "stricken ones" include such as Ben Zomah, who was stricken with insanity when he attempted to penetrate the mysteries of the *Merkava*. This Psalm was meant to protect the ascending mystic against such mishap.[75]

Another Psalm, which, according to the Zohar, was used especially to evoke the prophetic spirit, is the seventh Psalm.[76] This Psalm is called a *Shiggayon*, and according to at least one Midrash, this name is related specifically with the quest of the spirit of enlightenment and prophecy.[77] This would also explain the meaning of the mysterious word *Shiggayon* (שִׁגָּיוֹן), which causes the commentaries much trouble. According to this interpretation, its base would be the single letter Gimel (ג), and it would thus be related to *Nagan* (נגן), "to play music," and *Hagah* (הגה), discussed earlier. It would thus be a Psalm used specifically for *Hagah*-meditation.

The fact that the context of this Psalm deals with the singer's enemies rather than higher spiritual concepts does not contradict this. These enemies actually refer to the *Klipot* and forces of Evil which form a barrier, endangering one who would climb the spiritual heights. The first step in ascending to the higher spiritual levels therefore involves passing through the domain evil, this being indicated by the "stormy wind, deep cloud and flaming fire" in Ezekiel's vision. The primary purpose of the *Shiggayon,* like *Hagah*-meditation, is to clear the mind of the mundane and overcome these "enemies." A major mystic and Kabbalist, Rabbi Joseph Gikatalia (1248–1305), explicitly writes that this was the purpose of all the Psalms.[78]

Of all the Psalms, however, the most interesting is the 119th Psalm. Even in structure, this Psalm is different than any other passage in the Bible. It is in the form of an alphabetical poem or chant, with eight verses for each letter of the Hebrew alphabet. There is one other thing that also strongly draws our attention to this Psalm. This is the fact that all the words which we have determined to refer to meditation and meditative states occur in this Psalm in a disproportionately high number.

One significant feature of this Psalm is the fact that each letter is repeated eight times. This becomes very important when one realizes the meaning of the number eight. Although this is discussed in a number of places, the clearest analysis has been made by the eminent Kabbalist and mystic, Rabbi Judah Low (1525–1609), the "Maharal" of Prague, famed as the maker of the Golem.

According to the Maharal, the number seven refers to the seven days of creation, and hence, this number always denotes the perfection of the physical world. The number eight is the next step, and therefore eight denotes one step above the physical. Whenever we find the number eight used, it is in reference to something that brings one into the spiritual realm.[79] Elsewhere, the Maharal states that this is precisely the significance of the eightfold repetition in the 119th Psalm.[80]

The Maharal speaks of the number eight with regard to circumcision, which is always performed when the child is eight days old. Sex involves some of man's deepest emotions and strongest desires. In giving Abraham a covenant related to the sex organ, prescribing it for the eighth day, God indicated that these emotions and desires would henceforth be used for the mystical quest of the Divine on a transcendental level.

Very closely related to this concept is the fact that the High Priest *(Cohen Gadol)* would wear eight garments while serving in the Temple.

It is significant to note that before giving Abraham the commandment of circumcision, God told him, "Walk before Me and be complete *(tamim)*" *(Genesis 17:1)*. This is also the key word in the first verse of this 119th Psalm: "Happy are those who are complete *(tamim)* on the way" *(Psalms 119:1)*.

The word *Tamim* (תָּמִים) denotes spiritual completeness, where one can attain the eighth level, above the mundane. Thus, after forbidding various occult practices favored by the pagan Canaanites, God said, "You shall be complete *(tamim)* with the Lord your God" *(Deuteronomy 18:13)*. As the renowned exegete, Rabbi Isaac Abarbanel, explains, the word Tamim has the connotation of true enlightenment and prophecy, as distinguished from spurious mystical states.[81]

According to some Kabbalists, the word *Tamim* is closely related to the word *Teomim* (תְּאוֹמִים), meaning "twins." [82] When a person is complete — *Tamim* — then he is like a "twin" to the Supernal Man — the "Man" that Ezekiel saw sitting on the Throne. An individual who reaches such a level is then worthy of communing with the supernal Forces.

This also explains the meaning of the Urim and Thumim. These consisted of twelve stones, set into the High Priest's Breastplate *(Choshen)*, and inscribed with the names of the tribes of Israel.[83] This Breastplate was one of the Eight Vestments worn by the High Priest in the Temple.

According to some, the Urim and Thumim also consisted of a parchment containing the 72 letter Name, which was placed in the Breastplate.[84] According to the Kabbalists, the names of the tribes and other words inscribed on the twelve stones also contained exactly 72 letters.[85] This is significant, since, as we have discussed, the 72 letter Name plays an important role in the attainment of the prophetic state.

We have already discussed how the word for the Breastplate, *Choshen,* has the connotation of a mystical experience and revelation. It is also significant to note that the Urim and Thumim could only be used by the High Priest when he was wearing all Eight Vestments.[86] In using the Urim and Thumim, the Priest would reach the eighth level, transcending mere physical perfection and entering the spiritual domain.

According to the Talmud, the Urim and Thumim were actually used as the subject of mystical contemplation. The High Priest would contemplate the stones of the Urim and Thumim, meditating until he reached the enlightened state of *Ruach HaKodesh.* He would then see the letters on the stones light up, spelling out the necessary message.[87]

This explains the meaning of the terms Urim and Thumim. The word *Urim* (אוּרים), clearly comes from the word *Or* (אוֹר) meaning "light." This indicates that the letters actually light up.[88] The word *Thumim* (תּוּמִים) is derived from the word *Tamim,* under discussion.[89] This indicates that the *Thumim* would bring the High Priest to the level of *Tamim,* the completeness and perfection implied by *Ruach HaKodesh.*

Thus, when the 119th Psalm speaks of those "Complete on the way" *(Tamim Derekh),* it is speaking of those who are seeking enlightenment and the transcendental experience. One gets a definite impression that it was actually a Psalm changed by people seeking enlightenment, perhaps even the disciples of the prophets in their quest of the prophetic experience. As such, it could have been a like a long mantra, chanted in a prescribed order until it brought the individual to a high meditative state.

In this context, it is significant to note that the Baal Shem Tov (1698–1760), founder of the Hasidic movement, made use of this Psalm. He was taught by his spiritual Master that if he said the 119th Psalm every day, he would be able to speak to people, while at the same time maintaining a transcendental state of attachment to the Divine.[90] Thus, even among the later mystics we find that this Psalm played an important role.

Once we understand the meaning of the terms relating to meditation and the meditative state, we can accurately translate this Psalm. It immediately becomes evident that many passages are highly suggestive of the mystical experience. The Psalm speaks of the person walking the path of enlightenment, seeking higher states of consciousness, while at the same time asking to be delivered from error and other dangers facing those who ascend this spiritual heights.

THE URIM AND THUMIM

לוי רהם	שמעון ב	ראובן א
זבלון ח	יששכר צ	יהודה י
גד שבטי	נפתלי ב	דן ק יעק
בנימין	יוסף ון	אשר ישר

Levi RHM	Simon B	Reuben A
Zebulun Ch	Issachar Tz	Judah Y
Gad ShBTY	Naphtali B	Dan K YAK
Benjamin	Joseph UN	Asher YShR

◇ ◇ ◇

FROM THE 119TH PSALM

In Your mysteries I meditate *(siyach)*
And I gaze at Your paths;
   In Your decrees I am enraptured *(shasha)*
   I forget not Your word;
Ripen Your servant
I will live and watch Your word;
   Uncover my eyes, I will behold
   Wonders from Your Torah.[91]

.   .   .   .

Let me understand the way of Your mysteries,
I will meditate *(siyach)* in Your wonders;
   my soul melts from meditation *(tugah)*
   Support me as Your Word;
Remove me from a false way,
Favor me with Your Torah;
   I have chosen a way of faith,
   Your judgments make me stoic;
I have bound myself to Your testimonies,
O God, let me not be deceived;
   I run the way of Your commandments,
   For You have expanded my heart.[92]

8

The Meditators

The only expression that we have not yet discovered in the Bible is the one most commonly used by later writers in speaking of meditation, namely, *Hitbodedut*. It would be very disappointing not to find even a hint of this word, or usage in the entire Bible. On closer examination, however, this term, or at least a derivative of it, can indeed be found. In fact, this may be the original Biblical term for one who engages in meditation.

As discussed earlier, while the prophets themselves were very reticent when it came to openly discussing their techniques, clues can be found from other occult groups mentioned in the Bible, who often attempted to emulate the prophets. It is with one such group that we find the term "meditator." The prophet Isaiah speaks of such "meditators" when he says, "He overturns the signs of the meditators *(badim)*, He makes the diviners mad" *(Isaiah 44:25)*. Rabbi Ibn Ezra, a major commentator, explains the word *Badim* (בַּדִּים), saying, "This word comes from the root *Badad* (בָּדָד) (meaning isolation), since there are souls that have the power of meditate *hitboded)*.[93]

According to Ibn Ezra, the proper term for a "meditator" is the word *Bad* (בַּד). This is a shorter form of the later term which would be *Mitboded* (מִתְבּוֹדֵד), derived from the word *Hitboded*. This clearly indicates that meditation played an important role in the pagan occult services, just as it did among the prophets.

Among the occult practices forbidden in the Bible was a type of necromancy known as the *Oab* (אוֹב).[94] It was to such a necromancer that King Saul went when he wished to communicate with the soul of the Prophet Samuel.[95] It is most significant that the Targum translated *Oab* as *Bidin* (בְּדִין), again from the root *Bad*, indicating a "meditator." When Maimonides describes the practice of the *Oab*, it also appears to involve a type of mantra meditation, through which the necromancer attains a meditative trance necessary to commune with the dead.

This is particularly striking when we look at a verse that we have already mentioned. Isaiah speaks of, "Necromancers *(Oab-ot)* and mediums *(Yedonim)*, who meditate *(hagah)* and chirp *(tzaftzaf)*" *(Isaiah 8:19)*. We have discussed the word *Hagah* at length, and to a large degree, it has the connotation of a type of meditation that involves the chanting and repeating of a mantra. Here we clearly see that this was a method used by occultists involved in the *Oab*.

The word *Tzaftzaf* (צְפַצֵף) is interpreted by many commentaries to mean "chirp," the sound made by a bird.[96] As such, it would be an onomatopoetic word, reproducing the sound of a bird's twittering. However, it is significant to note that in two of the four times that the word *Tzaftzaf* occurs in the Bible, it is in conjunction with the word *Hagah*, which refers to meditation.[97]

According to the grammarians, any word which has a double base refers to an act repeated over and over in rapid succession. This is true of the word *Tzaftzaf*, and it therefore would denote a rapidly repeated sound. From the context, it would appear that *Tzaftzaf*, as practiced by the necromancers, involved the repetition of a sound over and over again, as in certain types of mantra meditation. The difference between *Hagah* and *Tzaftzaf* might be that the former is primarily the repetition of a word or phrase, while the latter involves an inarticulate sound.

This same idea is also found in another place, in which the prophet says, "Your voice shall be like a necromancer *(Oab)* from the earth; from the dust your words shall chirp *(tzaftzaf)"* *(Isaiah 29:4).* Here again we find that *Tzaftzaf* is associated with the *Oab,* indicating that it was normally used by such occultists.

A major Hebrew lexicographer, Rabbi Nathan ben Yechiel (1035–1106), states that the word *Tzaftzaf* has the connotation of both meditation *(Hagah)* and prophetic vision.[98] As such, it is closely related to the word *Tzofeh* (צוֹפֶה), meaning a "seer" or prophet. This in turn comes from the root *Tzafah* (צפה), meaning to "see," particularly in a prophetic or mystical sense.

The Root *Tzafah* also has the meaning of covering *(Tzipeh),* and in this respect is closely related to the root *Tzafan* (צפן) meaning to "hide" or "conceal." A prophet *(Tzofeh)* is one who sees, but what he sees is covered and concealed from the rest of humanity. This root is also closely related to *Tzuf* (צוף) meaning to "float," and in this respect a *Tzofeh* engages in a process very much like that discussed in the context of *Siyach*-meditation. The prophet not only sees, but he also floats and rises to a level above the mundane world.

This word may also be related to the root *Tzafaf* (צפף), meaning to "crowd" or "press." The seer must push his spirit against the body, pressing it out of the physical realm.

This last relationship is especially important, since the term *Tzaftzaf* is also used in this sense in a number of places in the Talmud and Midrash. Speaking of a person near death, the Midrash says, "the soul presses *(tzaftzaf)* to leave the body." [99] The Talmud likewise speaks of those in Gehenna, who "press *(tzaftzaf)* to ascend." [100] The Midrash also speaks of the final redemption as "breaking forth" *(tzaftzaf)*[101] From all these sources, it appears that the term *Tzaftzaf* refers to a sort of spiritual pressure, where one breaks through to a higher level. sensed by the mind.

The word *Tzaftzaf,* is used primarily with respect to the pagan cults, especially the *Oab.* These are the mystics who must exert spiritual pressure, pushing and shoving to break through to the spiritual. The true prophet, however, is on the level of *Siyach*, where by using the proper methods, he is able to float effortlessly to the highest realms.

◇ ◇ ◇

SOURCES

An individual involved in an *Oab* stands and burns a special incense, holding a myrtle wand in his hand and waving it. He speaks very slowly, repeating certain secret incantations. Asking a question, he hears something like the voice of another person speaking to him, answering the question in a very low voice. It is as if this voice is not heard by the ear, but only sensed by the mind.

Moses Maimonides.[102]

◇ ◇ ◇

Divination *(Kosem)* involves other methods used to entrance the mind and clear it of all thought. One is then able to predict the future, give advice, and warn against danger.

Some diviners make use of sand and stones. Some bow down *(gahar)* on the ground, making certain motions and loud sounds. Some gaze at a crystal or iron mirror and speak while in a trance.

Still others hold a staff in their hand, and lean on it, tapping it until their mind is cleared, whereupon they speak. Regarding this practice, the prophet said, "He asks his tree, and his staff tells him" *(Hosea 4:12)*.

Moses Maimonides[103]

◇ ◇ ◇

The diviners meditate *(hitboded)* in their thoughts, fixing their full concentration and all their emotions on the subject that they wish to know. As a result of their powerful meditation *(hitbodedut),* their mind is divested of all physical concepts. Their soul then communes with spiritual entities who can inform them of events in the near future.

Sefer HaChinukh (13th Century).[104]

◇ ◇ ◇

Through the meditation *(hitbodedut)* of Saul's imagination, his thoughts were aroused to recall what Samuel had said to him many times, that God would tear away his kingdom . . . [So vivid was this experience that] it actually seemed as if Samuel were speaking to him. This is the low voice that one engaged in an *Oab* nears, and regarding this it is written, "your voice shall be like an *Oab* from the earth" *(Isaiah 29:4)*.

This is actually like a hallucination, such as those experienced by the sick and feebleminded. It is therefore taught, that the inquirer hears the voice, but the occultist who raises [the dead person] sees, but does not hear.[105] This is because the occultist meditates *(hitboded)* on the [dead person] who is to be raised, and the power of his imagination causes him to see something that actually does not have any objective existence.

Rabbi Isaac Abarbanel.[106]

9

The Transition

One thing that we see clearly is that the forbidden idolatrous and occult practices very closely resembled the mystical practices of the prophets. This may have been one reason why the prophetic practices were concealed as hidden mysteries, restricted to relatively small societies. This was particularly true after the close of the prophetic period, where these practices were virtually unknown outside of very small, select circles.

The prophets knew that many people who did not have the proper preparation or temperament would attempt to emulate their practices. When unsuccessful, these people would turn to the relatively simple, but forbidden, meditative practices of the idolators. The prophetic methods were therefore shrouded in virtually absolute secrecy, and there is no express mention of them whatsoever in the entire Bible.

The Talmud states that during the prophetic period, there existed a literal "lust for idolatry." [107] It may seem somewhat difficult to understand how people could have a lust for something like idolatry, which, according to the context, was as strong as the sexual desire. But when there were many people involved in the mystical experience, the desire to join them was very strong. The mystical experience is one of the sweetest, profoundest, most uplifting experiences possible, and is something that can be very greatly desired.

At the same time, however, the true mystical experience is *Ruach HaKodesh,* which can only be attained after one has completed the ten preliminary levels. Before one can reach this level he must literally be a saint, both in his relationship to God and his dealings with man. Beyond this, one could not even enter the prophetic schools until he had undergone years of discipline and purification. People were therefore tempted to take shortcuts, and among the most readily available were the occult practices of the idolators.

During the time of Solomon's Temple, the Talmud informs us that there were literally millions of individuals involved in the prophetic mysteries.[108] It is no coincidence that idolatry and sorcery were so prevalent at the time. People who could not reach the spiritual heights of the prophets took the easy way of idolatry and occultism instead. It is therefore also no coincidence that when the prophetic schools were abolished after the destruction of Solomon's Temple, the "lust for idolatry" was also abolished.[109]

Still there were small closed schools that kept the traditions of the prophets alive. In order to prevent the masses from once again turning to idolatrous practices as a substitute for true prophetic meditation, they restricted the spread of these ideas. Finally, outside of a small school, these practices were totally unknown. The only ones who had any idea of the methods was a small, restricted school of Kabbalists.

Maimonides writes that prophecy will have to be restored before the coming of the Messiah.[110] As we have seen, however, prophecy does not occur automatically, but must be cultivated with extensive discipline through very specific practices. Before the Messianic age, therefore, these practices will have to be revealed and taught. Only then will there be a fulfilment of the prophecy, where God said, "After that, I will pour out my spirit on all flesh, and your sons and daughters will prophesy. Your old men will dream dreams, and your young men will see visions" *(Joel 3:1).*

◇ ◇ ◇

בְּנֵלֶךְ וּלֹאאֵיִ תּוֹשְׁלְבֵּעַ

Notes

Part One: The Traditions

1. In its earliest use, the word *Hitboded* has this sense. See *Ekhah Rabbah,* introduction 20. Also see *Chovot HaLevavot, Shaar Cheshbon HaNefesh* 3 #17 (53a), *Shaar HaBechinah* 6, *Shaar HaYichud* 8; Radak, *Sherashim, YaRaD, EChaD; Otzar Nechmad* on *Kuzari* 3:1 (3a). See *Mesilat Yesharim* 15, 26, where it is also *apparently used in this sense. Cf. Chovot HaLevavot, Shaar HaPerishut* 2.

2. *Shaarey Kedushah,* Park Four (British Museum #749, f. 15b). A similar expression is found in *Likutim Yekarim* (Jerusalem, 1974) #29, 38.

3. *Milchemet HeShem* 2:6 (Riva di Trento, 1560, p. 19a).

4. Aldous Huxley, *The Doors of Perception* (Harper, Row, New York, 1970) p. 22f. *See* my article, "On Immortality and the Soul," *Intercom* 13:2 (May, 1972), p. 5 (published by the Association of Orthodox Jewish Scientists).

5. This entire analysis is taken from *Sefer HaMaspik LeOvday HaShem* (Jerusalem, 1965) p. 177 ff. This is a translation from the Arabic *Kefayah Al-e'abdin,* done by Yosef ben Tzalach Dori. Although the translator's use of the word *Hitbodedut* is not certain, a similar Arabic word is likewise translated by Ibn Tebon in the *Guide to the Perplexed.*

6. *See* Rashi and Ibn Ezra on these verses. *Cf. Moreh Nebukhim* 1:18.

7. *See* Ibn Ezra *ad loc.* In Hebrew, "soul" and "spirit" are respectively *Nefesh* and *Ruach.* As we shall see, revelation is primarily through *Ruach.*

8. *See* Isaac of Acco, *Meirat Eynayim, Ekev.* This has been

8. See Isaac of Acco, *Meirat Eynayim, Ekev.* This has been published by Adolph Jellinek in *Philosophie und Kabbalah* (Leipzig, 1854) p. 48. It is also quoted in *Shaarey Kedushah*, Part Four 17a. Also see *Chovot HaLevavot, Shaar Yichud HaMaaseh* 4 (Warsaw, 1875) p. 12a; *Maggid Mersharim, BaShalach,* 15 Shevat 5311 (Jerusalem, 1960) p. 57a; *Keter Shem Tov* (Kehot, New York, 1972) *220, Likkutim Yekarim* 179. Also see Yehudah Albotini, *Sulam HaAliyah* 10 (Jerusalem, Ms. 334 8°), published by Gershom Sholem in *Kitvey Yad BaKabbalah* (Jerusalem, 1930) p. 226.

9. See *Rashi,* Radak, *ad loc.*

10. *Cf.* Ibn Ezra, Radak, *ad loc.*

11. Cf. *Tamid* 32b, *Yad, Talmud Torah* 3:13. The Hebrew word for "meditate" in this verse is *Ranan*, which is discussed at length in Part 3:4.

12. *Iggeret HaMusar* (Warsaw, 1927) p. 7.

13. *Yad, Yesodey HaTorah* 7:4, quoted below, Part 2:4.

14. *In the original Arabic, Maimonides uses the same word for meditation, "self isolation," as does his son Abraham. In their translations of Moreh Nebukhim (Guide to the Perplexed), both Samuel Ibn Tebon and Judah Al-chrizi render this word as Hitbodedut. Ibn Tebon's translation was seen, and possibly edited by, Maimonides himself.*

15. *Bereshit Rabbah* 10:7. Cf. *Zohar* 1:251a, *Zohar Chadash* 4b.

16. Quoted in commentary of Rabbi Moshe Botril on *Sefer Yetzirah* 4:2.

17. *Ibn Ezra, commentary on Psalm 92:5. Also see commentary on Exodus 20:8, Micah 2:1; Yesod Moreh 8.*

18. Commentary on Deuteronomy 13:2.

19. *Tur, Orach Chaim* 98. Also quoted in *Shulchan Arukh, Orach Chaim* 98:1. See *Toldot Yaakov Yosef, Acharey* (Koretz, 1780) p. 88c.

20. *Pardes Rimonim,* commentary on *Bava Metzia* 59b (Sabbioneta, 1554) p. 4a.

21. *Sefer HaIkkarim* 2:25 (Warsaw, 1871) p. 90b.

22. *Sheelot UTshuvot HaRadbaz* 967 (3:532). The reference is to *Rabbi Jacob of Marvege (c. 1170–1230), in Sheelot UTshuvot min HaShamayim* #58.

23. Quoted in Sefer *Cheredim, Tshuvah* 3 (Jerusalem, 1958) p. 214. Also quoted in *Beer Halachah* on *Orach Chaim* 571:2 *"Talmid Chacham."*

24. *Sefer Cheredim, loc. cit.* (p. 215). The Talmudic reference is *Berakhot* 5:1 (30b). The quotation is very much like one found in

Shaar HaKavanot LeMekubalim HaRishonim (Florence, Ms. 41, p. 222a, b; Vatican, Ms. 31, p. 37; Munich, Ms. 240[8], British Museum, Ms. 777[4], Perma, Ms. 86[7]; Jewish Theological Seminary, New York, Ms. 1833, p. 33). This is also quoted in *Shaarey Kedushah,* Part Four (British Museum, Ms. 749) p. 18b. This has been published, together with a German translation by Gerhard Scholem, *"Der Begriff der Kawwana in der alten Kabbala,"* MGWJ 78:511 (1934).

25. *Metek Sifasayim* 30.

26. *Tzavaat HaRivash* (Kehot, New York, 1975) #8; *Likutim Yekarim* 38. Some attribute this to Rabbi Dov Baer, the Maggid of Mezrich.

27. *Avodat HaKodesh, Tziporen Shamir* 51. Also see *Midbar Kadmut, Heh* 13. The author cites an interesting allusion from *Leviticus 16:4, where the word Bad,* meaning "linen," is related to the word *Hitbodedut.* He also notes that the initial letters of the verse, "In all your ways know Him" *(Proverbs 3:6),* spell out *Badad.*

28. *Likutey Moharan* 52.

29. *Etz Chaim, Shaar TaNTA* 5, from Psalm 23:31. *Also see* HaGra on *Sefer Yetzirah* 1:9, *Nefesh HaChaim* 1:15.

30. *See* Ramban *ad loc. Cf. Zohar* 3:123b. Also see *Shefa Tal,* Introduction (Hanau, 1612) p. 4b; *Likutey Amarim* (Tanya) 1:2.

31. *Shaar HaGilgulim* 1.

32. *Avodah Zarah* 20b, *Sotah* 9:15 (not in Gemorah), *Yerushalmi, Shabbat* 1:3 (8b), *Shekalim* 3:3 (14b), *Shir HaShirim Rabbah* 1:9; *Machzor Vitri* 937, *Sefer Chasidim* 16, *Reshit Chakhmah, Shaar HaAhavah* 11.

33. This is available in two English translations, the most reliable being that of Shraga Silverstein, published by Phillip Feldheim, Inc.

34. *Shaarey Kedushah,* Part Four (at end of printed edition).

35. *Tana DeBei Eliahu Rabbah* 2. Cf. *Tana DeBei Eliahu Zuta* 1.

36. *Mekhilta* on Exodus 14:31.

37. *Tana DeBei Eliahu* 9.

38. See *Shaarey Kedushah* 3:7.

39. *Yad, Yesodey HaTorah* 7:1. This contains an allusion to the ten steps noted in note 32. A full English translation of this can be found in my *Maimonides Principles* (National Conference of Synagogue Youth, New York, 1975) p. 33ff.

40. *Derekh HaShem* 3:3:1–4. My translation, *The Way of God,* is published by Phillip Feldheim, Inc. (New York, 1977).

Part Two: The Prophets

1. *Rashi on Exodus 1, Rashbam on Genesis 20:7. This, however, is strongly disputed by Ibn Ezra on Exodus 7:1, Rashi, Bava Kama* 60a "Niv."

2. *Yeriot Shlomo,* Volume 1; Dihernfurth, 1788), p. 96a. See *Bava Batra* 12a, regarding Psalms 90:12.

3. Commentary on Genesis 20:7, Exodus 7:1, Numbers 11:25.

4. *Cf.* Psalms 19:3, 49:8, 78:2, 119:171. *See* Radak, *Sherashim.*

5. See *Avodah Zara* 4b, *Likutey Amarim* (Tanya) 1:1.

6. In the ten steps, mentioned in part 1, note 32, we thus find that *Ruach HaKodesh* brings the resurrection of the dead.

7. Ezekiel 37:4, 9, 12.

8. *1 Kings 20:35; 2 Kings 2:3, 2:5, 2:7, 2:15, 4:1, 4:38, 5:22, 6:1, 9:1. See* Targum *ad loc.*

9. *Yad, Yesodey HaTorah* 7:2–7.

10. *Derekh HaShem* 3:3:5–3:4:1.

11. *Mesekhta Atzilut* 5, *Pardes Rimonim* 19:2,3. *Cf.* Zohar 3:92a, *Tikuney Zohar* 6b. *See* Isaac of Acco, *Otzar HaChaim* (Guenzberg Ms. 775) pp. 92b, 112a, 116a.

12. *Mekhilta,* Rashi, on Exodus 19:18, *Tanchuma, Yitro* 13, *Bereshit Rabbah* 27:1, *Kohelet Rabbah* 2:24.

13. *Mesekhta Atzilut* 14. In the writings of many earlier Kabbalists, *Chesed* (Love) is called *Gedulah* (Greatness), and *Yesod* (Foundation) is called *Kall* (All).

14. *Zohar* 2:37a, *Avodat HaKodesh, Tachlit* 42. Cf. *Moreh Nebukhim* 1:11.

15. Rabbi Moses Cordevero, *Shiur Komah* 21.

16. *Yad, Yesodey HaTorah* 7:6, *Moreh Nebukhim* 2:34.

17. Malbim *ad loc., Shiur Komah* 22. Cf. *Tana DeBei Eliahu Rabbah* 31 (120b).

18. *Chagigah* 2:1 (11b), 13a. From *Hekhelot Rabatai* we see that this referred to practice and not mere theory.

19. *See* Ibn Ezra, Radak, *ad loc., Chagigah* 13b.

20. *Hekhelot Rabatai* 21. A translation of the text will appear in *Meditation and Kabbalah.*

21. *Zohar* 2:81a, 2:131a, 2:203a, 3:227a, *Pardes Rimonim* 25.7, *Shaarey Orah* 5 (Warsaw, 1883) p. 50b. These confuse the mind. See *Zohar* 3:123a, *Tikuney Zohar* 11b, *Reshit Chakhmah, Shaar HaYirah* 4 (16c).

22. *Cf.* Job 40:6, 1 Kings 2:1, 11.
23. Radak, Abarbanel, *ad loc.,* from *Devarim Rabbah* 7:8. See Rashi, *Chagigah* 13b *"Kall," Moreh Nebukim* 3:6.
24. *Torat HaShem Temimah* (in *Kitvey Ramban,* Jerusalem, 1963) p. 168.
25. See *Minchat Shai* ad loc., Ibn Ezra, Recanti, Tzioni, on Exodus 14:19.
26. Particularly in *Chayay Olam HaBah* and in *Sefer HaCheshek.* This system is also discussed as length in *Shaarey Kedushah,* Part Four. It is mentioned by Rabbi David ben Zimra (Radbaz), *Magen David, Vav.*
27. *Bahir* (Jerusalem, 1951) #94, 107, 110; *Zohar* 2:270a, Rashi, *Succah* 45a "Ani," *Pesikta Zutrata* on Exodus 33:21. It is vocalized in *Pardes Rimonim* 21:5. For an explanation of this Name, see *Raziel HaMalakh* (Margolies edition) p. 54ff.
28. Commentary on Ezekiel 1:4.
29. *Minachot* 29b. The word *Mazal* does not occur in our texts.
30. This idea is taken from *Shaarey Orah* 3,4 (37b). *See* note 106. It is quoted directly in *Shaarey Kedushah,* Part Four 20a.
31. *See* Rambam, *Shemonah Perakim* 1.
32. *See* Rambam, Commentary on *Sanhedrin* 10:1, Seventh Principle; *Yad, Yesodey HaTorah* 7:6.
33. This is detailed in *Hekhelot Rabatai* 16-25. See *Zohar* 2:102b.
34. *Bereshit Rabbah* 82:7, 47:8, *Zohar* 1:213b, 3:182b, 3:217a, 3:262b.
35. *Megillah* 14a. The 600,000 individuals mentioned there parallel the 600,000 who left during the Exodus.
36. *Yoma* 9b.
37. *Shaarey Kedushah* 3:5, 6.
38. Exodus 25:18–22, 40:18.
39. Deuteronomy 31:26, Rashi *ad loc., Bava Batra* 14a. See Radak, Ralbag, Abarbanel, on 1 Kings 8:9.
40. *Shekalim* 6:2, *Tiferet Yisrael* ad loc., *Yad, Bet HaBechirah* 4:1. See *Yoma* 52b, *Horiot* 12a, *Keritot* 5b; *Tosefta, Yoma* 2:13, Tosefta, Sotah 13:2, *Yerushalmi, Shekalim* 6:1 (24b), *Seder Olam Rabbah* 24; *Kuzari* 3:39 (48b); Rashi, Radak, Ralbag, on 2 Chronicles 35:3. For a discussion whether the ark was concealed or carried off to Babylon, see *Yoma* 53b. It is also debated if it was hidden under the Holy of Holies or in the Chamber of the Woodshed. See *Yoma* 54a.
41. *Derashot HaRan* 8 (Jerusalem, 1974) p. 128, *Avodat HaKodesh, Sitrey Torah* 4:25. *Cf. Bereshit Rabbah* 70:8.
42. *See also* Numbers 7:89.

43. Abarbanel on 1 Samuel 3:3, quoted in "Sources." This may be the reason why God was said to "dwell among the Cherubs" (1 *Samuel 4:4, 2 Samuel 6:2), and to "ride on a Cherub" (Psalms 18:11, See* Targum *ad loc.*). See *Ma'arekhet Elokut* 12 (163b).

44. *Succah* 5b, *Chagigah* 13b. *See* commentaries on Exodus 25:18.

45. *Mekhilta* on Exodus 20:20.

46. *Moreh Nebukhim* 3:45, *Chazkuni* on Exodus 25:18.

47. The Cherubs are therefore seen as the angels of Gehenna, through which one must pass before entering Paradise. *See* Targum J., Bachya, on Genesis 3:24.

48. See *Midrash HaGadol,* Ramban, Bachya, Tzioni, Hirsch, on Exodus 25:18, *Tanchuma, VaYakhel* 7, *Moreh Nebukhim* 3:45, *Zohar* 1:32b.

49. Commentary on Exodus 25:21.

50. Commentary on 1 Samuel 3:3.

51. *Ralbag, Abarbanel on 2 Kings 3:15.*

52. *Shaarey Kedushah,* Part Four 15b.

53. *Livnat HaSapir,* quoted in *Abodat HaKodesh, Takhlit* 10.

54. *Yeriot Shlomo,* Volume Two (Roedelheim, 1831) p. 22b. *See also* Volume One, p. 76b. Cf. *Moreh Nebukhim* 3:45.

55. *Shaarey Orah* 1 (4a). *See* Isaiah 18:5; Rashi on Exodus 15:2, Isaiah 25:5; Radak, *Sherashim,* ZaMaR.

56. *Likutey Moharan* 64:5, from Song of Songs 4:8, Hirsch on Genesis 49:22.

57. *Likutey Moharan* 3. Cf. *Zohar* 3:223b, *Zohar Chadash* 26d, 48a.

58. *Yad, Yesodey HaTorah* 7:4.

59. Quoted in the sources in Part 1:4.

60. *Derekh HaShem* 3:4:2, 4, 9, 10.

61. *Yerushalmi, Berakhot* 1:1.

62. Abraham Abulafia, *Chayay Olam HaBah* (Jewish Theological Seminary, Ms. 2158) p. 18a, quoted in Jellinek, *Philosophie und Kabbala,* p. 44; Judah Albotini, *Sulam HaAliyah* 10 (*in Kitvey Yad BeKabbalah,* p. 227), *Shoshan Yesod Olam* (Sasoon, Ms. 285) 343, 501, 1003.

63. *Pardes Rimonim* 15:3. *Cf. Bahir* 138.

64. *Bahir* 138. *See* Ramban, Bachya on Exodus 17:11.

65. *Bahir* 124. See *Sefer Yetzirah* 1:3.

66. *Sefer HaCheshek* (Jewish Theological Seminary, Ms. 1801) p. 9a. This is quoted in *Shaarey Kedushah,* Part Four 12a.

67. *Berakhot* 34b. *See* sources at end of this section.

68. *Avodah Zarah* 17a. See also *Chasdey David* on *Tosefta, Berakhot* 2:15; Ibn Ezra on Job 32:19.

69. *VaYikra Rabbah* 31:4. This brings together the "covenant of the tongue" with the "covenant of the sexual organ." See *Sefer Yetzirah* 1:3.

70. *Kidushat Levi* ad loc. *See* note 57.

71. *Bava Metzia* 86b, Rashi on Genesis 18:4. There is one opinion that they worshipped the sun, and therefore bowed to the sand that was heated by it, *Shnei Luchot HaBrit, Torah SheBeKatav, VaYera* (3:27b). See also *Yafeh Toar* on *Bereshit Rabbah* 50:4, *Mizrachi, Gur Aryeh,* on Genesis 18:4.

72. *Tshuvah,* quoted in *HaKotev, Eyin Yaakov, Chagigah* 14b (#11), *Otzar HaGaonim* ad loc., *Chelek HaTshuvot* p. 14.

73. *Even HaShoham,* Introduction (Jerusalem, Ms. 4168°) p. 1b, quoted in Scholem, *Kitvey Yad BaKabbalah,* p. 90. The term, "vision and not allegory," is taken from Numbers 12:8. Tzayach uses this same expression in *Sheirit Yosef,* after the chant involving the Ten Sefirot. *See* following note.

74. *Sheirit Yosef* (Vienna, Ms. 260) p. 168a.

75. Jeremiah 11:21, 26:9.

76. *See* Recanti, Bachya, *ad loc. See also* Abraham Abulafia, *Mafteach HaShemot* (Jewish Theological Seminary, Ms. 1897) p. 58b.

77. *Midrash Tehillim* 91:8. The word "know" in this verse may also mean attachment, in the sense of "Adam knew his wife Eve" (Genesis 4:1).

78. *Sulam HaAliyah* 10, quoted in Scholem, *Kitvey Yad BaKabbalah,* p. 229.

79. *Shaarey Orah; Pardes Rimonim* 20; *Shnei Luchot HaBrit, Bet HaShem* (1:5a). *Cf. Avot Rabbit Nathan* 34:2.

80. *Kiddushin* 71a, *Zohar* 1:1a, 2:17b, 2:234b, 3:256b; *Tikyney Zohar* 66b, 82b, 104a, 131b; Rashi, *Avodah Zarah* 17b *"Lama," Sanhedrin* 60a *"Shem,"* 101b *"U'VeLashon"; Tosefot, Succah* 5a *"Yud," Chagigah* 11b *"Ain," Avodah Zarah* 18a *"Hagah." See also* Rosh, *Yoma* 8:19, *Taam Zekenim* p. 55, *Tshuvot Bach* 293. These names are discussed in detail in *Pardes Rimonim* 21:9, 12.

81. *See* Notes 26, 27. See also *Avot Rabbi Nathan* 13:3, *Bereshit Rabbah* 44:22, *VaYikra Rabbah* 23:2, *Devarim Rabbah* 1:9, *Shir HaShirim Rabbah* 2:6, from Deuteronomy 4:34; *Tanchuma, VaYera* 4, *Pesikta* 5 (52b), *Zohar* 2:234b, *Tikuney Zohar* 8b.

82. *Sifsey Cohen* (Shakh), *Yoreh Deah* 179:18, *Be'er HaGolah* (Maharal) 2 (Warsaw, 1928) p. 11a. For examples, see *Yebamot* 49a, *Gittin* 68b, *Sanhedrin* 95a, *Bekhorot* 8b, *Shemot Rabbah* 1:35, Rashi, Ramban, on Exodus 2:14; *Kohelet Rabbah* 3:15, *Midrash Tehillim* 36:8, Rashi on Isaiah 29:12, Jeremiah 21:4; *Midrash Tehillim* 91:8, *Pesikta* 19 (140a).

83. *Sanhedrin* 10:1 (90a), *Avodah Zarah* 18a, *Pesikta* 22 (148a); *Tosefta, Sanhedrin* 12:1, *Yoreh Deah* 179:8. See also *Midrash Tehillim* 91:8 (200b), *Tosefta, Yadayim* 2:9, HaGra *ad loc.* #25, R. *Shimson (Rash), Yadayim* 4:8. Also see Judah Albotini, *Sulam HaAliyah* 9 (Jerusalem, Ms. 1302 8) p. 15b, (Jerusalem, Ms. 334 8) p. 96a; Quoted by Gershom Scholem, *Kiryat Sefer* 22:170 (1945).

84. *Or Yakar,* Commentary on *Zohar Shir HaShirim* (Jerusalem, Ms. 74 4°), quoted in *Kitvey Yad BaKabbalah,* p. 235

85. *Sotah* 38a, *Sifri,* quoted in *Tosefot* ad loc "Harey," *Yalkut* 1:879. *See also* Rashi, *Mekhilta,* on Exodus 20:21.

86. The *Lishkat HaGazit,* the Chamber of the Great Court *(Sanhedrin). See* Rashi, *Taanit* 16a "Horah," *Agadat Bereshit* 14:3, *Targum Sheni* on Esther 4:1.

87. *Sotah* 7:6 (38a), *Tamid* 7:2 (33b), *Yoma* 3:8 (35b). The response is derived from Nehemiah 9:5. See *Berakhot* 63a, *Taanit* 16a, *Sotah* 40b.

88. *Avot* 5:5, *Yoma* 21a; *Bereshit Rabbah* 5:6, *VaYikra Rabbah* 10:9. *Cf. Avot Rabbi Nathan* 35:8.

89 *Yoma* 39a, Rashi *ad loc.* "MiLeVarekh," *Minachot* 109b, *Tosefta, Sotah* 13:8, *Tosefot, Sotah* 38a "Harey," *Yad, Tefillah* 14:10. *See also* Rashi, *Eruvin* 18b "MiYom."

90. *Kidushin* 71a, *Yerushalmi Yoma* 3:7 (18b), *Kohelet Rabbah* 3:15, *Zohar* 3:146a, *Yad, Avodat Yom HaKippurim* 2:6, *Or Zerua* 2:28a, *HaGra, Orach Chaim* 5:1 "VeYiKaven."

91. *Or HaSekhel* 9:1 (Vatican, Ms. 233) p. 112b. See *Moreh Nebukhim* 1:62.

92. *Hekhelot Rabatai* (in Wertheimer, *Batey Midrashot,* Jerusalem 1893) 16:4 (Vol. 1, p. 92). See also *Razo shel Sandelfon,* in *Markava Shlemah* (Jerusalem, 1922) p. 4b.

93. *Chayay Olam HaBah,* quoted in Note 62; *Sefer HaCheshek,* quoted in Note 66; *Or HaSekhel* 8:3 (109b), quoted in *Pardes Rimonim* 21:1, *Sulam HaAliyah* 9, quoted in Scholem in *Kiryat Sefer* 22:167 (1945).

94. This is discussed at length in *Shaar Ruach HaKodesh.* A complete discussion will be found in *Meditation and Kabbalah.*

95. *Pardes Rimonim* 21:1. The letter combinations in the illustration are quoted there, taken from "Sefer HaNikkud." This is actually *Or HaSekhel,* cited in Note 93. See *Or Yakar,* Commentary on *Zohar Shir HaShirim,* quoted in Scholem, *Kitvey Yad BaKabbalah,* p. 232.

96. *Pardes Rimonim* 30:3. This is quoted in *Shaarey Kedushah,* Part Four, 10a.

97. *Avot* 1:13, *Avot Rabbi Nathan* 12:13, *Yoreh Deah* 176:16 in *Hagah,* 245:21 in *Hagah.*

98. See Note 82, 83.

99. *Cf.* Rashi, *Avodah Zarah* 17b *"Lamah," Sanhedrin* 101b *"U'VeLashon," Tosefot, Berakhot* 7a *"HaHu," Sefer Chasidim* 205, 484, *Ikkarim* 1:18, *Tshuvot Rashba* 1:220.

100. *Derekh HaShem* 3:2:5, 6, 7.

101. *Mekhilta* on Exodus 12:1, Rashi, Radak, on Jeremiah 45:3, *Avodat HaKodesh, Sitrey Torah* 25.

102. Commentary on *VaYechi* (Lvov, 1880) p. 37d, quoted in *Minchat Yehudah* (Chayit) on *Maarekhet Elokut* 10 (Mantua, 1558) p. 143b. Also quoted in *Shaarey Kedushah,* Part Four, p. 18a. The first paragraph here follows the reading in *Shaarey Kedushah,* rather than the printed edition, since the former is more explicit.

103. *Or HaShem* 2:4:4 (Vienna, 1860) p. 46a.

104. *Magen Avot* 2:2 (Livorno, 1785) p. 16a.

105. Commentary on 1 Samuel 10:5.

106. *See* Note 30.

107. This is discussed at length in *Sulam HaAliyah* 7, quoted by Scholem, *Kiryat Sefer* 22:162 (1945). *See also* Abraham Abulafia, *Otzar Eden HaGanuz* (Bodleian, Ms. Or 606) pp. 16a, 17a.

108. *Avodat HaKodesh, Sitrey Torah* 27 (Warsaw, 1894) p. 135c,d.

109. *Shiur Komah* 16 (Warsaw, 1883) p. 30d.

110. *Mekhilta* on Exodus 12:1, *Sifri* on Deuteronomy 18:15, *Tanchuma* Bo 5, *Midrash Tehillim* 132:3, Rashi, Radak, on Jonah 1:3, Ramban on Deuteronomy 18:15. *Zohar* 1:85a, 1:121a, 2:170b, *Emunot VeDeyot* 3:5, *Kuzari* 2:14, Ibn Ezra on Joel 3:1, *Tshuvot Radbaz* 2:842, Radal on *Pirkey Rabbi Eliezer* 10:11. The only one who apparently disputes this is Rabbi Abraham Abulafia. See *Sefer HaCheshek* (Jewish Theological Seminary, Ms. 1801), p. 32a. Maimonides also does not mention this.

111. *Yoma* 9b, *Kuzari* 2:24 (40a).

112. *See* end of Part Three, Notes 107 and 109.

113. *Chagigah* 2:1 (11b).

114. *Likutey Moharan* 3. *Cf. Abudraham* (Jerusalem, 1963) p. 126.

115. *Barakhot* 33a. Note that it was also the Great Assembly who banished the lust for idolatry. *See* Note 112.

116. *Megillah* 17b.

117. Paraphrasing *Succah* 45b.

118. The "Early Saints" *(Chasidim Rishonim)* are mentioned a number of times in the Talmud. See *Berakhot* 5:1 (30b), *Nedarim* 10a, *Bava Kama* 30a, *Niddah* 38a, *Simachot* 3:10, 12:8, *Bereshit Rabbah* 62:2. The Pharisees *(Perushim)* are also mentioned, see *Yadayim* 4:6, *Chagigah* 2:7 (18b), *Tosefta Shabbat* 1:15, *Shabbat* 13a, *Sotah*

22a, Kiddushin 66a; R. Yitzchak ben Malchizedek, Bertenoro, on *Damai* 2:3. *See also* Josephus, *Autobiography* 2, *Antiquities* 13:5:9, 18:1:3, *Wars* 2:8:14. Although the Pharasees are frequently maligned, they were among the greatest saints and mystics of their age.

    19. Parapharsing Numbers 11:25.

    120. Paraphrasing Isaiah 17:6.

    121. Paraphrasing Jeremiah 3:14.

    122. Paraphrasing Isaiah 41:17.

    123. Paraphrasing Daniel 9:24.

    124. See Sefer Chasidim 205, 206.

    125. Paraphrasing Isaiah 28:7.

    126. *Chagigah* 14b. This is discussed at length in *Meditation and Kabbalah.*

    127. *Ibid.* 15b.

Part Three: Verbal Archeology

1. *Cruden's Concordance* lists the following. From the root *Siyach:* Genesis 24:63, Psalms 77:12, 104:3, 119:15, 23, 48, 78, 97, 99, 148, 143:5. From the root *Hagah:* Joshua 1:8, Isaiah 33:18, Psalms 1:2, 5:1, 19:14, 49:3, 63:6. It is significant to note that *Hagah* occurs translated as meditation only in the first two books of the Psalms, while *Siyach* occurs in this context only in the last three books. The second book ends, "This concludes the prayers of David son of Jesse" (Psalms 72:20). Also note the disproportionate number of times the word *Siyach* occurs in Psalm 119.

2. *Berakhot* 26b. See *Tosafot, Avodah Zarah* 7b "*VeAin.*"

3. Commentary *ad loc.* Regarding Hagar, *see* Genesis 16:14. Some however, maintain that Isaac actually meditated in Jerusalem. See *Pesachim* 88a, Rashi *ad loc.* "*Har,*" *Tosefot, Berakhot* 34b "*Chatzif.*"

4. Such as Psalm 69:13, Job 21:4.

5. *Chagigah* 5b, from Amos 4:13; *Sotah* 44b, *Minachot* 36a.

6. *Yeriot Shlomo,* Volume Two (Roedelheim, 1831) p. 12a. This is quoted in part in *HaKatav VaHaKabbalah* on Genesis 24:63. *See* Deuteronomy 28:63, Psalms 52:7, Proverbs 2:22, 15:25.

7. *Shabbat* 82a. As such, the root *Nasach* (נסח) is related to the word *Nashah* (נשה), meaning to "forget."

8. *See* Rashi, Radak, *ad loc.; Sefer Sherashim* "*NaSaCh.*"

9. *Succah* 28a.

10. *Arukh, "Sakh"* (סח). See *Beer Mayim Chaim,* quoted in *Etz Yosef* on *Eyin Yaakov, Succah* 7.

11. *Tikuney Zohar* 70 (125b).

12. Commentary on Genesis 2:5, 24:63, Psalms 55:18, 64:2, 102:1. *See* Ibn Ezra on Genesis 2:5.

13. *See especially, Zohar* 1:25b, *Tikuney Zohar* 51 (86b).

14. See *Shemot Rabbah* 1:9. See also *Kehillat Yaakov, "Sneh."* Abulafia also constructs a mandala representing the Burning Bush out of 120 Alefs, See *Sefer HaCheshek* (Jewish Theological Seminary, Ms. 1801) p. 12a. The figure there actually should be that of a truncated triangle.

15. For a general discussion regarding the relation between a Tree and the Sefirot, see *Shaar HaPeskukim* (Tel Aviv, 1961), p. 5. Regarding climbing the Sefirot, *see* Part Two, Note 30.

16. Ibn Iera on Genesis 2:5. *See also* Hirsch on Genesis 1:11

17. *Bereshit Rabbah* 53:13. *Cf. Bereshit Rabbah* 13:2.
18. See *Shaarey Kedushah* 3:5, quoted above, Part 2:2.
19. *Zohar* 2:60b. This is the Sefirah of Kingship *(Malkhut)*.
20. *See* Rabbi Samuel Tzartzah, *Makor Chaim* on Exodua 3:2 (Mantua, 1559).
21. *Bahir* 176, *Zohar* 3:24a. The *Etrog* is *Malkhut*, the Palm frond *(Lulav)* is *Yesod*, the three myrtle twigs are *Chesed, Gevurah, Tiferet*, while the two willows are *Netzach* and *Hod*. See also *VaYikra Rabbah* 30:14.
22. *Yerushalmi, Succah* 5:1 (22b), *Tosefot, Succah* 50b "Chad."
23. See *Megillah* 14a, Rashi on Genesis 11:29; *VaYikra Rabbah* 1:3, Targum on 1 Chronicles 4:18, *Niddah* 24b. See *Likutey Moharan* 21:3.
24. Radak on Psalm 119:1, Ibn Ezra on Psalm 119:4.
25. *Yeriot Shlomo,* Volume One (Diherenfurth, 1784) p. 19b.
26. *Ibid. See* Exodus 28:15.
27. *See* Note 87.
28. See *Chagigah* 13b, *Arukh* "Chashmal." See also *Etz Chaim, Shaar HaTzelem* 3 (Tel Aviv, 1960, p. 51), *Shaar HaChashmal* 1 p. 291), *Shaar Kitzur ABYA* 6 (p. 401), *Mavo Shaarim* 6:2:3, *Shaar HaKavanot, Inyan Levishat Begadim* (Tel Aviv, 1962) pp.12, 13, *Pri Etz Chaim, Shaar HaTfillah* 3 (Tel Aviv, 1966), p. 19. See *Shaarey Kedushah* 3:6, quoted above in Part Two #2, that the Chashmal is a "Garment."
29. See Part Two, Note 34.
30. Commentary on Joshua 1:8. *See also* commentary on Psalms 1:2, 63:7, 37:30. Rashi is an acronym for Rabbi Shlomo Yitzchaki-Yarchi.
31. *Kohelet Rabbah* on 1:16.
32. Commentary on Psalms 1:2, 9:17.
33. *Sherashim, HaGaH.*
34. See Part Two, Note 92.
35. *Sanhedrin* 10:1 (90a). *See* Part Two, Note 83.
36. *Eruvin* 21a, *Avot Rabbi Nathan* 25:1, commenting on Ezekiel 2:10. This verse, however, is particularly speaking of the World to Come. See *Arkhin* 13b.
37. *Berakhot* 17a.
38. *Yeriot Shlomo,* Volume One, p. 99b.
39. See *Republic,* Book Six (488).
40. Commentary on Psalms 9:17; *Jeshurun* 8:118.
41. *Yeriot Shlomo,* Volume One 77b, Volume Two 22b. See also *Torah Or* (Kehot, New York, 1972) p. 37a.
42. *Hekhelot Rabatai* 24:4. *HaAderet VeHeEmunah,* found in the prayer book, is a similar chant. *Ibid.* 28:1.

43. *Hekhelot Rabatai* 16, 17. The text is quoted in *Meditation and Kabbalah.*

44. *Zohar* 1:4a.

45. *See* Part Two, section 5.

46. On 1 Kings 18:42, however, the Targum merely translates *Gahar* as *Gachin,* which means "to bow."

47. *See* Rashi, Ibn Ezra, Hirsch *ad loc., Sefer Sherashim,* "LaHaH," *Arukh, "Lah." See also Yeriot Shlomo,* Volume One, 106b. The word *Gahar* (גהר) may thus be a combination of the roots *Hagah* (הגה) and *Harhar* (הרהר), which means "to think" or "to ponder."

48. See *Meditation and Kabbalah.*

49. *Yeriot Shlomo,* Volume Two 22b, Hirsch on Psalm 33:1.

50. *See also* Isaiah 14:7, 42:9, 44:23, 49:13, 55:12, Psalm 98:4.

51. *Midrash Tehillim* ad loc.

52. *Yad, Yesodey HaTorah* 2:2. *See* Sources.

53. *Or Torah, MiKetz* (37a). Cf. *Likutey Torah, BaHaAlotekha* (30a), *VeEtChanan* (8a); *Siddur* (of Rabbi Shneur Zalman of Liadi) pp. 48a, 51d, 278c.

54. *See* Psalms 118:15, Proverbs 11:10.

55. *Devarim Rabbah* 2:1.

56. *Devarim Rabbah* 2:1.

56. *Shaarey Orah* 1 (4a).

57. *Sefer Shershim,* "ShUA". See *HaKatav VeHaKabbalah* on Genesis 4:5, Radak, Hirsch on Psalms 94:19, Rashi on Psalm 119:16. *See* Rashi, Radak, on Isaiah 29:9.

59. See *Zohar* 2:85b, 2:118a, 2:162b, 2:165a, *Tikuney Zohar* 70 (131a), *Nefesh HaChaim* 1:6, *Likutey Amarim (Tanya)* 1:4.

60. See *Gesenius' Hebrew Grammar* (Bagster, London) 55:4 (p. 93).

61. *Sefer Yetzirah* 1:6. See *Midrash Lekach Tov* on Genesis 1:1 (Vilna, 1884) p. 1b.

62. *Likutey Moharan* 24.

63. *Chagigah* 14a, *Sanhedrin* 93b, Rashi on Exodus 31:3, R. Yonah, Bertenoro, on *Avot* 3:17.

64. *Yad, Yesodey HaTorah* 2:2.

65. *Yad, Tshuvah* 10:3.

66. *Cf.* Rashi on 1 Kings 3:21, 43:18.

67. Job 11:6.

68. *Kuntres HaHitbonenut.*

69. Ecclesiastes 10:13, 1:17, 2:12, 7:25, 9:3. *Cf.* Isaiah 44:25.

70. Commentary on 2 Kings 9:11.

71. *Pesachim* 117a, *Midrash Tehillim* 24. The Psalms that begin with *Mizmor LeDavid,* and were therefore used to attain inspiration

were therefore, Psalms, 3, 4, 5, 6, 8, 9, 12, 15, 22, 23, 29, 38, 39, 62, 63, 65, 141, 143. See *Zohar* 1:39b, 1:67a, 1:71a, 1:87a, 1:123b, 2:140a, 2:170a, 3:123b.

72. *Midrash Tehillim* 90:4. See *Pesikta* 31 (198a).

73. *Shabbat* 15b, Maharsha *ad loc.*, *Yerushalmi, Shabbat* 6:2, *Eruvin* 10:11.

74. *BaMidbar Rabbah* 12:3, *Tanchuma, Nasa* 27, *Midrash Tehillim* 91:1.

75. Hai Gaon, quoted in Part Two, Note 72. See *Shaarey Orah* 1 (3b).

76. *Zohar* 2:45a.

77. *Midrash Tehillim* 7:3. *Cf.* Habakkuk 3:1, Psalm 9:17. Some interpret *Shiggayon* to mean ecstasy. *See* R. Jonah ibn Ganach, *Sherashim* "ShaGaH."

78. *Shaarey Orah* 1 (3b).

79. *Tiferet Yisrael* 2.

80. *Ner Mitzvah* (Bnei Brak, 1972) p. 21.

81. Commentary on Exodus 27:30. *Cf.* Bachya *ibid.*

82. *Shaarey Orah* 5 (41a). See *Shir HaShirim Rabbah* on 5:2.

83. Exodus 28:30. *See* commentaries *ad loc.*

84. *Zohar* 2:234b. *Cf.* Targum Yonatan, Rashi, Bachya, Recanti, on Exodus 28:30, Ritva, *Yoma* 73b.

85. Bachya, Chazkuni, *Baal HaTurim* on Exodus 28:21; Abraham Abulafia, *Mafteach HaChakhmot* (Jewish Theological Seminary, Ms. 1686) p. 104b. The names of the twelve tribes contained fifty letters. An addition 22 letters, which also completed all the letters of the alphabet, was obtained by adding the words, "Abraham, Isaac, Jacob, *Shivtey Yeshurun*"

אברהם יצחק יעקב שבטי ישורון

See *Yoma* 73b. Each stone thus contained six letters.

86. Rashi, *Yoma* 71b *"BaElu."*

87. *Yoma* 73b, *Yad, Kley HaMikdash* 10:11.

88. *Yoma* 73b.

89. *See* Note 81.

90. *Shivechey HaBaal Shem Tov* (Jerusalem, 1969) p. 98.

91. Psalm 119:15–18.

92. *Ibid.* 119:27–32.

93. Others say that they are called *Badim* because they wear linen garments. *See* Sherashim, *Bad.* Others say that it is because they are false, from the word *Bada* (בדא). *See* Rashi, Ibn Ezra, on Isaiah 44:25, from Job 11:3. A relationship between the *Badim* here and the word *Badad* (isolation) may be found in the Talmud, *Berakhot* 63b, *Taanit* 7a, *Makkot* 10a.

94. Leviticus 19:31, 20:6, 20:27, Deuteronomy 18:11.

95. 1 Samuel 28:3–9.

96. Rashi on Isaiah 8:18, 29:4, *Sherashim, "Tzaftzaf,"* from Isaiah 10:14. See *VaYikra Rabbah* 6:6, Rashi on *Rosh HaShanah* 16a, *Sotah* 12b.

97. The four places are Isaiah 8:18, 10:14, 29:4, 38:14.

98. *Arukh "Tzaf,"* From *Sotah* 12b, based on Isaiah 8:18. *See* Abraham Abulafia, *Otzar Eden HaGanuz* (Bodleian, Ms. Or 606) 9a.

99. *VaYikra Rabbah* 34:2.

100. *Rosh HaShanah* 17a. The *Arukh, "Tzaf,"* states that *Tzaftzaf* here means "swimming or praying," from the root *"Tzaf," meaning "to float." Rashi, however, interprets it as meaning "to scream."*

101. *Shir HaShirim Rabbah* on 6:10.

102. *Yad, Avodat Kokhavim* 6:1. See *Sanhedrin* 65b; *Sefer HaMitzvot,* Negative Commandments 8, 9, 31.

103. *Yad, Avodat Kokhavim* 11:6. See *Sifri* on Deuteronomy 18:10. Malbim *ibid.* states that this is like an Ouija Board. See also *Sefer Mitzvot Gadol (Smag),* Negative Commandment 52.

104. *Sefer HaChinukh* 510. This is attributed to Rabbi Aaron HaLevi of Barcelona.

105. *Midrash Samuel* 24.

106. Commentary on 1 Samuel 28:7, fourth opinion. This is the opinion of Rabbi Levi ben Gershon on 1 Samuel 28:8.

107. *Yoma* 69b, *Sanhedrin* 64a.

108. *Megillah* 14a, *Shir HaShirim Rabbah* 4:22, *Ruth Rabbah* 1:2.

109. Rabbi Elijah, the Gaon of Vilna (HaGra), commentary on *Seder Olam* 29 (Jerusalem, 1971) p. 99. See *Meshekh Chakhmah* on Numbers 17:17, (end of *BaHaAlotekha),* who derives this from Zechariah 13:2. The Talmud, *Yoma* 69b, states that when the Evil Urge was captured, it was seen to emerge from the Holy of Holies. As discussed above, however, this is the place of the Cherubs, the source of prophecy. The Cherubs were thus both the source of prophecy and the source of the lust for idolatry. If contemplating the Cherubs could bring about a prophetic state, people mistakenly assumed that other images could be substituted. See also *Torat Chaim,* quoted in *Etz Yosef,* in *Eyin Yaakov, Yoma* 69b.

110. *Iggeret Teimon* (Warsaw, 1927) p. 30. See also *Yad, Melachim* 12:2.

INDEX

Hebrew

Bible Quotes